Mama had a quote for every situation:

"We shouldn't judge another's knitting till we've knitted at least two perfect socks ourselves...."

"Give a spoonful of love and you'll be paid a cupful brimming over!"

"It must be a comfort to You, Lord, that we earthen vessels can iron out a few wrinkles in our relationships with each other. It will save You a mite of work when we step into heaven."

Betsey Jennings

# MAMA'S PATHWAY to HEAVEN

## Alice J. Kinder

 LIVING BOOKS

Tyndale House Publishers, Inc., Wheaton, Illinois

The following chapters have appeared elsewhere in revised form:

Chapters 1, 3, and 8 in *The War Cry* (The Salvation Army, 860 N. Dearborn St., Chicago, Ill. 60610)

Chapter 4 in *The Lighted Pathway* (Church of God Publishing House, 1080 Montgomery Ave., Cleveland, Tenn. 37311)

Chapter 5 in *The Standard* (The Nazarene Publishing House, Box 527, Kansas City, Mo. 64141)

Chapter 7 in *The Kentucky School Journal* (Kentucky Education Association, 101 W. Walnut, Louisville, Ky. 40202) and *The Appalachian News Express* (Box 802, Pikeville, Ky. 41501)

All Scripture references are taken from the *King James Version* of the Bible, unless otherwise noted.

First printing, August 1983

Library of Congress Catalog Card Number 83-70616
ISBN 0-8423-4030-0

To the memory
of my mother
and all who, with
their feet of clay
and love for others,
walk the Christian
path to heaven

# Contents

# ❦ Mama's Parlor Bedroom

"The guest room is ready to welcome
visitors!" Mama announced contentedly
the day she finished papering the new
parlor bedroom. It was wallpapered in a
lovely pattern of trailing pink roses and
had two shiny glass windows.

Separated from the parlor by an oak
door with a glass pane, the room held
a handsome four-poster bed that Uncle
Pettigrew had made. Beside the bed stood a
small table he had carved from prime maple
wood. Beyond the table stood an ancient
clothes rack that had once belonged to
Great-grandmother Greenleaf.

Made of heavy iron, the clothes rack had
a big circle at the top to hold hangers. It was
an antique with the nicks to prove it, and
must have served many people. My
brothers and I used to wonder about the

many events witnessed by that old piece
of furniture.

"Jenny, the parlor bedroom needs
dusting," Mama coaxed one hot summer
afternoon. I went about doing as she had
asked, but I dreaded the ordeal of gliding
the dust cloth in and out of all the tiny
grooves in the iron clothes rack. That was
why I left that part of the job until last.

"Mama," I later told her in disgust, "it gave
me the creeps to squeeze the lint out of all
those tiny dark holes!"

"Any task worth its salt requires more
than a spoonful of work," my energetic
mother replied, quoting one of her favorite
sayings.

"But, Mama, . . ."

Just then there was a noise outside.
"Someone's at the gate!" Mama declared.
"Never can tell, Jenny. The parlor bedroom
may be used tonight. . . ."

I ran to the porch, where a tall boy
around eighteen years old greeted me.
He had black curly hair and walnut-brown
eyes. Something lay hidden in his eyes—
an indefinable mystery or sadness.

The boy reached for his pack of notions
and other merchandise. He was a drummer
boy, the third to pass through Deep Valley

that summer. By then Mama had come out
to see who our visitor was.

"These scarves are nice," he told Mama
shyly, his voice distinctly crisp, unlike the
accent in our hill country.

"They are indeed," she said, her voice
softly melodious. "But we can't buy
anything today."

"That's right, Betsey," Papa affirmed,
as he stepped onto the porch. "Hello there,
boy. You've quite an assortment, I see."

"But I can't sell anything," the boy
murmured dejectedly. "I've journeyed all
over these hills."

"I'm sorry, son. We'd buy if we could.
We don't buy many luxuries here."

"Will," Mama said brightly, "the boy must
spend the night with us. Maybe things will
seem better in the morning."

Papa noticed the uncertain, dark clouds in
the sky. "A storm is brewing," he remarked.
"Sure, the boy must spend the night."

"Storms give me an eerie feeling," the
drummer boy commented, his dark eyes
filled with apprehension. "The wind. . . ."

"God is our refuge and strength, a very
present help in trouble," Mama assured
him, quoting Aunt Hannah's favorite psalm.

With a start the boy looked down at her

calm face. "Therefore will not we fear," he quoted, "though the earth be removed, and though the mountains be carried into the midst of the sea."

"Why, you know the Old Testament, too!" cried Mama in delight. "What's your name, boy?"

"Nathaniel Finklehoffe, a Jewish name. My parents held the psalms in high esteem."

But in spite of his parents' respect for the psalms and his own knowledge of them, the boy must have forgotten their comforting promises. That night he tied two sturdy new scarves to our ancient clothes rack and attempted to hang himself. Clayton found him just in time.

The next morning everyone remained quiet around the breakfast table. Even the fresh new rays of sunlight dancing radiantly through the panes failed to lift the gloom. Hardly anyone spoke after Papa asked the blessing.

As she cleared the table, Mama remarked thoughtfully, "Nathaniel, you can't travel on today. So why not stop with us awhile?"

Papa observed the rain-soaked garden and fields. "The corn will need to be straightened and hoed. We could use extra help."

"I've never done farm work," Nathaniel

replied slowly. "But I'll do my best,
Mr. Jennings."

"Doing one's best is all the Lord asks,"
Mama said briskly. "It's the choice way to
spend time and much better than merely
marking days from the calendar."

"Your practical wisdom reminds me of
my mother," Nathaniel murmured wistfully.

That evening he told us about his parents.
When I heard the story, I realized why his
eyes were sad, as if they'd never held a
happy thought, and why he'd tried to leave
the world.

His father and mother had come from
Germany to America. He and his two
brothers had been born in Pennsylvania.
A closely knit relationship had held the
family together until one windy, bleak
November day when a burly fellow entered
his father's store.

"A confounded Jew!" the husky man had
exclaimed angrily. "No one can make a
living here since you foreigners came."

Mr. Finklehoffe had restrained his temper
despite the stranger's increasing taunts. But
when the intruder insulted his wife, he
could hold back no longer. In the fight that
followed, he was knocked through the
window and died on the pavement outside.

"Mother lived only a year after that," Nathaniel said slowly. "She tried to hold the business together. Everything was against us, though. No one had any use for us because of the competition and our religion."

Mama, who loved all people and whose heart held no corner for prejudice or hate, looked up at the boy. "Christ was a Jew," she said softly.

"My people are still looking for the Messiah," Nathaniel said reflectively.

"The Savior has already come," Mama replied with assurance.

The next day rain fell again—this time a soft pattering kind caressing the attic roof. "The very day to clean house," Mama decided.

A thoughtful look appeared in her blue eyes. "Will, let's put the wardrobe Pettigrew made in the parlor bedroom instead of in our bedroom. We'll move the clothes rack someplace else."

"Move the clothes rack!" Papa exclaimed, as if the event were unthinkable. Then his eyes alighted on Nathaniel. "Why, of course, Betsey, the wardrobe should go in your parlor bedroom."

"But where will we put Grandmother's clothes rack? She used to tell us that she had brought it over from Old England."

"On the ship?" Nathaniel asked in disbelief. "But it's so heavy."

"I've always doubted the tale myself," Mama quipped. "In her old days Grandmother got events tangled up sometimes. She probably picked it up at an auction in North Carolina."

"Betsey," Papa said, "let's take the rack to the lean-to room off the kitchen."

"But, Will, how can we get it through the door?"

The boys and Papa pushed and tugged on the heavy rack. At the threshold of the lean-to room they came to an abrupt halt. The big round top wouldn't fit through the doorway.

"What now?" Mama asked.

"Mrs. Jennings, I believe this top lifts off," observed Nathaniel from his tall height. "Why, so it does!"

He turned hard on the center of the rack. To our amazement, he lifted the round top completely from the rack!

In further astonishment, we watched as he pulled a small folded paper, crinkled with age, from the hole in which the top had been secured.

The Jewish lad read slowly from the paper: "'But these are written, that ye might believe that Jesus is the Christ, the Son of God; and that believing ye might have life through his name. John 20:31.'"

"Why, that's a clipping from an old **War Cry**!" Mama cried. "Grandmother's folks used to send her those papers from England."

"What's the **War Cry**?" Nathaniel asked.

"A magazine published by the Salvation Army folks. Grandmother said they were good people who did kind acts for others. She said they'd stop people right in the street and tell them about the Savior."

"The Savior," Nathaniel said thoughtfully. "Thank you for moving the rack out of the bedroom, Mrs. Jennings. And may I have this paper? It's from your Bible, isn't it?"

As the days passed, the boy began reading the Bible. He started asking questions about Jesus and discussed religious ideas with my parents.

When he left the next spring, Mama's parlor bedroom remained lonely without an occupant a long time. And then one day Uncle Nathan came from Chicago to visit us. He told us that a group of Salvation Army people would stop at our county seat the next Christmas. He urged us to ride into town to hear them.

We went, of course, and were pleased
with the service. The message was on the
love of Jesus Christ. "These are written, that
ye might believe that Jesus is the Christ,
the Son of God; and that believing ye might
have life through his name," began the tall,
black-haired young speaker.

His dark eyes searched the crowd as if he
were looking for someone. Clutching Papa's
sleeve, Mama uttered a low cry of delight.
It was Nathaniel Finkelhoffe.

After the meeting she expressed her full
pleasure. "Oh, Nathaniel!" she cried happily,
running to hug the young man as if he were
one of my four brothers.

She turned to greet the two young men
nearby, who looked exactly like Nathaniel.
"Your brothers, of course!"

"Yes," Nathaniel replied proudly. "All
three of us are working for the Salvation
Army and with Christ's help are trying to
do our best."

"Any task worth its salt requires more
than a spoonful of work," quoted Mama,
using her favorite rule for successful labor.
"No one has to succeed—he has only to try.
That is, if an inner urge from the Holy Spirit
spurs him on."

She stopped to observe the Christmas

spirit among the Salvation Army workers. The snowflakes fell onto the sidewalk as softly and easily as a sigh.

"How wonderful that you boys have accepted Christ and are serving Him!" Mama declared with delight.

"From her small height she looked up and gave the trio of fine young men a grateful smile.

"The three of you are going home with us tonight," she told them. "Home to Deep Valley and our parlor bedroom."

# ❀ Mama's
# Blue-speckled Teapot

The visit of the Finklehoffe brothers made
us realize that many people work to spread
the Christian gospel. We worked hard the
next spring planting our crops. Each night
in our devotional hour we prayed for a
bountiful harvest. With a good harvest, we
would be able to increase our weekly tithe
in church on Sunday.

"God needs our money for the growth
of His work," Mama told us. "After our
tithe, we can spend money to buy clothes
and necessities for the house."

One of the first necessities Papa bought in
the fall was a new teapot. Mama delighted
in her shiny new aluminum teapot. Still,
she couldn't bear to throw her leaky blue-
speckled one away. It had been a wedding
gift from Papa, a part of our family life
down through the years.

"Will, we'll hang the old teapot behind

the pantry door," Mama decided, her eyes intent on the faded blue flecks. "I'll think of a purpose for it later."

Papa nodded assent. Busy with his pencil and a strip of brown wrapping paper, he was absorbed in figuring the yield of our harvest corn. "The Lord has truly sent a blessed season this year," he spoke at last. "With a full harvest we'll have enough to meet our needs and our portion for Him, of course."

A swiftly dawning light leaped into Mama's eyes.

"Why, that's what we'll use the teapot for—as a new place for setting aside our tithe!" she exclaimed with joy. "Only yesterday I wondered what we'd use after I dropped Grandma's sugar bowl."

Papa gave an indulgent smile. After all, teapots and sugar bowls weren't such important matters. What mattered was that God's portion be used to lead people to the Lord.

Mama returned Papa's smile and began scrubbing her blue-speckled teapot for its new role. Working away, she sang "Brighten the Corner Where You Are." To her, such items as teapots and corners were vital necessities for living. She felt that God was also interested in the role of little things;

otherwise He wouldn't have made people so dependent on them.

That afternoon my brothers and I admired Mama's work in sprucing up the ancient teapot. "Perhaps it would look better hanging by the kitchen window," she decided on impulse. "More light will filter in on it there."

"We'll put our tithe in the teapot every week, won't we, Mama?" My brother John planned ahead.

"Then we'll take it to church on Sundays," my other brother Clayton said.

Each week we deposited our tithe in the teapot. The boys and I took turns counting our church money.

"Betsey," said Papa one Saturday afternoon, "do you have anything extra in the cupboard? Let's visit Jonah Malone today. He's pining away since Samantha died."

Mama reached to check the cupboard shelves. "And Samantha pined away over little Celia's drowning in the mill pond," she commented. "Of course, Jonah had to keep that water in store to run his mill. They still blamed themselves for their child's death."

When we visited Mr. Malone, we found him on the porch. He thanked us for the food and seemed glad to see us. Yet when

Papa invited him back to church, he stalked
the floor in sudden anger.

"Don't talk about God and church
attendance to me!" he exclaimed heatedly.
"What has God ever done for me—except
take my family?"

At that outburst Mama quickly ushered
the boys and me to the gate. Papa followed.

"I do wish we could lead Jonah to depend
on the Lord in his need," Papa said on the
way home. "But not even a mountain can
move him to faith, it seems."

"Um," Mama said, lifting her left
eyebrow in thought. She looked up at the
gray-shadowed sky. "Rain is in the making.
And a regular storm, I'd say, by the
tumbling clouds."

That night the lightning and the thunder
took turns racing across the sky. Rain
poured down in a streaming avalanche.
On Sunday morning the creek was up to
our walk log. Papa feared that the bridges
below us had washed away.

By eight o'clock he and the boys were
able to wade through the water. It seemed
an eternity before they returned with the
news. The lock on Mr. Malone's mill pond
had broken loose and the overflow had
flooded the church!

"We can't take our tithe to church today," Clayton observed, as he looked toward Mama's blue teapot. "So we'll have two tithes for next week, won't we, Papa?"

"Yes, son. That is, if we can get the debris cleaned out of the church by then. And the bridges repaired so we can get to meeting."

"Will," Mama said, "for some reason I keep thinking of Jonah alone in his dreary old house. Somehow I have a certain feeling about him."

When Papa and Clayton called on Mr. Malone, they found him sick in bed. He'd come down with a cold from checking his stock in the storm, he said. Papa knew he shouldn't be left alone, as sick as he was. Papa also remembered Mama's "certain" feeling. Adding the two together, he knew there was only one thing to do—bring Jonah Malone home to stay with us. It was a good thing, too. He had pneumonia, we soon discovered.

While Mama and I cared for Mr. Malone, Papa, the boys, and others cleaned the church and repaired the bridges. By the next Sunday everyone could return to church. All except Clayton, who would stay with our guest.

Mr. Malone watched us take the tithes

from the teapot. "Samantha had a teapot like that one," he said in a thoughtful voice. "She set great store by it."

Mama's left eyebrow lifted slightly. "Your wife set considerable store by her church attendance, too," she added rather tartly. "I'm sorry, Jonah," she quickly apologized. "I just wish you were going with us. If only you would wash the window of your soul to let God's love shine through!"

The sick man looked up at her. His glance wavered and he turned to look out the window. We left him staring through the sunlit panes.

That evening during our devotional hour, Papa read Leviticus 27:30: "'And all the tithe of the land, whether the seed of the land, or of the fruit of the tree, it is the Lord's: it is holy unto the Lord.'" He glanced at our teapot, then knelt to thank God for the yield of our land that had enabled us to fill it.

Before long, Mr. Malone was able to walk about the house. One evening he stood near the enamel teapot, his eyes fixed on its blue flecks.

"Will, I'll be going home soon," he said at last. "Before I leave, there's something I must tell you and your family." He hesitated. "It's really terrible—what I have to say."

Mama looked up from her mending. Her left eyebrow raised in thought as she remembered the "certain" feeling she'd sensed all along about their neighbor.

"We're your friends, Jonah," she encouraged him.

"You are indeed. And from living with you two, I've discovered my need for a greater Friend." Mr. Malone's voice sank low. "I'm going to church next Sunday to confess my sin and ask God's forgiveness."

He sat with his chin in his hands. "Betsey," he said, "your reminding me how Samantha liked her meetings made me remember the value she set on church attendance. And then there was your teapot, too."

"My teapot?"

"Yes. It kept reminding me how much we owe our Maker—despite everything. The thought made me see my loss differently. But about my sin. . . ." Mr. Malone watched the flames by the fire. "On the night of the storm I let the pond loose so it would—flood the church."

Unable to believe the tale, all seven of us stared at Jonah Malone.

"Yes, I was that bitter toward God for taking my family," he continued. "Since then I've lain awake nights, asking for mercy and forgiveness."

"Papa cleared his throat and lifted his right hand to his chin in a thoughtful gesture. Mama lifted her left eyebrow in meditation. She brushed a misty tear from her blue eyes.

"All of us need forgiveness for one sin or another," she spoke in an understanding tone. "As my grandmother used to say, we shouldn't judge another's knitting till we've knitted at least two perfect socks ourselves or sat in his place by the hearth a whole week."

Mr. Malone smiled briefly. "Betsey, you have such a gift for molding everyday routine to fit Christian principles."

He looked around the room. "The warmth and hospitality in this kitchen are enough to warm the whole world."

Mama sat silent for once, not heeding the mending in her lap.

Mr. Malone stood beside the mantel. "I'm going home to find Samantha's teapot to use as a tithing one just like yours," he declared. "Except that I'll owe the Lord a considerable number of past installments. You see, I can't ever repay God for the mercy He's shown in my guilt."

"Two tithing teapots!" Mama exclaimed, smiling up at Papa. "Sometimes little things, rather than mountains, may be used to lead people to the Lord," she mused softly.

Standing tall beside her, Papa nodded in agreement. He smiled at her before turning to watch the firelight glow, which shone radiantly on the teapot.

# 🐾 Mama's Oldest Brother

Mama came from a big family of nine brothers and sisters. When her sister Careen died, it broke her heart. Aunt Careen had been the oldest in the family. Next in age was Uncle Nathan, a favorite brother. He was used to city ways and was always in a hurry.

"He doesn't have time to consider his soul and the Lord's Book," Mama sighed more than once.

At Aunt Careen's funeral my brother Clayton declared, "Uncle Nathan never took his time like this before." A tinge of amazement flavored his assertion.

As Clayton stood beside the bright array of flowers around the casket, I tightly held his hand. Aunt Careen must have been loved by almost everybody in Deep Valley, I decided, since so many people had brought flowers.

Several of the women carried bright, crinkly crepe-paper flowers they often made for such occasions, but a great number had been aware of the natural floral beauty created on our hillsides. Vases of white trillium blooms, fragile violet petals, and blossoms of yellow honeysuckle filled almost every space available. Near the window Uncle Aaron had placed fragrant bowls of lilacs from the bush that Aunt Careen had once planted by their doorway.

Only one vase of flowers had been ordered from a floral shop. We had no floral shops in our town. The store-bought flowers had come all the way from a big town up near the Great Lakes. Uncle Nathan had brought them with him on the train the night before.

Loosening my grasp of Clayton's hand, I turned to a little girl who looked about nine years old—the same age as I. Above our heads the tall grown-ups stood in groups, talking softly. They moved here and there to greet newcomers, and the women cried as they hugged each other. The crowd above was so dense I couldn't see the faces.

But I could see Uncle Aaron's face. He sat immovable near the lilac blooms. His face reminded me of big Hat Rock on our high pinnacle above the house. It was all stony and marblelike. No one could peer beyond the wrinkles to see what hurt inside.

"He's taking it hard," a woman whispered.

Mama had also "taken it hard," I knew, because Aunt Careen had been a favorite sister. Mama had cried upon learning of my aunt's death. After a while, though, she'd reached for the Bible and read several verses. Moments later she had put on a clean apron and started down to help out at Uncle Aaron's.

"Work is the best patented medicine in the world to ease a heartache," she said.

While the adult voices sifted through the air, the little girl and I stared at each other. Her eyes were the color of crackling brown leaves in the fall. Yet they remained silent like a foggy morning. They held no answering word pictures, unlike the eyes of my brothers, which replied with whole sentences when they looked at me.

Tentatively I laid my hand on the little girl's fingers. After a moment she laid her hand on mine. I edged closer and placed my arm around her shoulder. In the midst of death we had found companionship.

Side by side we sat while the funeral service began. I couldn't understand all the preacher said. Yet I caught words that

sounded like the verses Papa read from the
Bible. When the preacher spoke of a time
to be born and a time to die, I remembered
what Mama and Clayton had said about
Uncle Nathan.

My uncle didn't share time with others
because he stayed busy making money. He
lived in a big northern city and owned three
stores. He and Aunt Netha didn't have any
children to care for, so they spent all their
time caring for the stores. Mama once said
she never saw anyone who could hurry
along as her oldest brother did.

At last, though, he didn't seem to be in
a hurry. Sitting with Mama and the rest of
the family, he was taking time to listen to
the sermon.

By this time the preacher was accenting
every syllable. He seemed to look directly at
each person in the room as he declared that
death was one thing you had to meet in real
life for yourself before it came alive for you.

In the past two days I had discovered that
death meant many things. It meant crying
and sad faces. It meant people coming and
going and relatives stopping to see Aunt
Careen. They hadn't taken time to visit her
when she lay sick. Death meant a lot of
singing and preaching and flowers for
someone who could no longer see them.

After the service the night before, Mama had said people of different ages showed their grief in different ways. "The loss of a loved one," she had reflected, "hurts so much that previous anxiety and fear thin down and trail unheeded through the door."

"Yes," Papa had agreed, "and death jolts us into remembering all the things we've considered tackling but somehow never got around to unrolling." He had lifted his right hand to his chin in a thoughtful gesture.

Both my parents believed that death was merely another chapter of life, the glorious chapter to be continued in the eternal life in heaven.

To me death meant Aunt Careen was lying white and still in a store-bought dress, one in which she wouldn't feel at home if she'd had anything to say about the matter. It meant that she and I would never gather eggs together again or search for yellow buttercups beside the spring near her washing kettle.

I looked around the room at all the people. Why, each of us would have to die some time—Papa, Mama, my brothers, and I. Even the little girl beside me. Perhaps we could sit near one another in heaven.

After we'd gone to the cemetery and left Aunt Careen covered all young and fleecy

gold beneath May sunlight, a crowd of
people went home to eat with us. The little
girl was among the group.

The two of us swung from the boughs of
the apple trees. We chased bright butterflies
near the lilac blooms. I finally learned her
name. It was Serena Lane, she said, and she
lived with her brother because her parents
were dead. But she didn't like it there much
because no one played with her. Her
brother worked in the mines; his wife
kept busy cleaning the house.

"Doesn't she ever play with you?" I
asked. "Why, Mama and Papa and the
boys take time to play with me."

Then I turned to see Uncle Nathan
strolling through the garden. It seemed
strange that he was walking slowly, as if
sifting his thoughts. Again, he appeared
in no hurry at all.

If he had never taken time before and
was doing so now, it had to be because
Aunt Careen had died. Maybe that was
what death did to people. It made them
think real hard about a great many things.
Maybe it had made Uncle Nathan wish he'd
come to see Aunt Careen while she could
still speak to him. Perhaps that was why he
was taking time at last to talk to his relatives
and stroll slowly through our garden.

Mama came out, and she and Uncle
Nathan talked about Aunt Careen and about
God and the Bible.

"Your religion isn't confined to an isolated
hour in your schedule, Betsey," Uncle
Nathan commented. "Rather, your faith
flavors all moments and situations."

"Oh, Nathan." Mama looked up at the
blue sky. "God's creativity is a radiant
blessing," she said. "His presence seems
so close today."

"I wish I knew the Lord as you do,
Betsey," Uncle Nathan said.

"Accept Him then," Mama said simply.

They stopped near the swing. My uncle
pushed Serena high into the air. Her eyes
lit up with pleasure. She looked pretty
now with the somber silence chased from
her face.

After Mama went inside, Uncle Nathan
took time to swing Serena and me in the
dwindling afternoon sunlight. He also took
time to tell us stories about life in the big
town where he and Aunt Netha lived.

"We get lonely sometimes, though," he
reflected quietly at last. "Your aunt would
love to have two little girls just like you. If
she did, why, I suppose she'd spend all her
time playing with them."

A twinkle appeared in his blue eyes so

similar to Mama's. "Then I'd have to work harder than ever in the stores," he said, laughing.

Serena smiled shyly. That afternoon she and Uncle Nathan had taken a special liking to each other. She hugged him good-bye when her sister-in-law came for her.

The next Christmas, Uncle Nathan brought Aunt Netha when he came to visit. She was so lovely I couldn't keep my eyes off her. Her own lively amber eyes took us all in simultaneously, or so it seemed, and her sprightly walk was somehow different from the way we were used to walking. Aunt Netha didn't talk as we did either, but we loved to listen to her voice because she was the kind of person who left the doorway open to conversation instead of shutting it.

"We've started going to church," she told Mama. "We're taking time at last. You see, Nathan and I want to know the Lord as you and your family do, Betsey."

"Accept Him then," Mama replied simply as she had once before. To her, religious faith wasn't a complicated matter at all because it encircled the heart.

Two days after Christmas, Serena Lane's brother was killed in the mines. Again people stopped to consider how precious

the gift of life is. And once more amid
death Uncle Nathan took his time.

Not worrying at all about the the three
stores and their big house, he and Aunt
Netha helped out at Lena Lane's for four
days. Afterward they took Serena back with
them for a visit, while Mrs. Lane went home
to her folks. In the spring they adopted
Serena and wrote to Mama.

"Oh, Mama," I exclaimed upon hearing
the news, "the first time I saw Serena, I
knew she was my friend! How wonderful
that she is my cousin now."

Mama smiled as she read aloud more of
Uncle Nathan's letter:

"Betsey, we enjoy our daughter's
companionship more each day. No home
is complete or as joyous without children.
We may adopt a brother for her soon.

Serena loves her Sunday school class
and the Bible stories we read her. Netha
and I accepted the Lord and were
baptized last Sunday. The only thing I
regret is that we let busy-ness and
business keep us outside the church
door so long. It kept us from having
a family, too."

Mama paused briefly to look at her
family. She felt inner peace and satisfaction;

her eyes contained a grateful prayer. Then she continued reading the letter:

"God plants an awareness of life and its meaning in each individual heart, I think. It's just that too many of us don't wake up to consider our sin, our souls, and the souls of others soon enough."

The letter was several pages long. Uncle Nathan must have had plenty of time to write so much about his conversion.

I was glad Mama wouldn't have to sigh over her brother again.

# 🌸 Mama's Path to Heaven

After Aunt Careen's death and Uncle Nathan's conversion, Mama took a few "ginning" days to talk to the Lord about heaven. She wanted all her family to accept Him so they could hold a family reunion in their eternal home.

"I must witness to them and others more than ever now," she said. "And share my faith with everyone, even though I stumble and fall daily."

Having come from a Primitive Baptist background, Mama had heard stories about the golden streets and harp-playing angels all during her childhood. With Aunt Careen moving away from earth to take member-ship in heaven, Mama now began to scrutinize such stories for the first time. As she thought of Aunt Careen's busy fingers always itching for the next task, she wondered if her sister would be happy walking golden streets and playing music.

"Careen never had any gold in this world, Lord," she confided. "She was happy without it. She'd feel more at home walking a country valley road with dandelions and violets trimming the path, but golden streets would be a wondrous sight to her. Careen never played music and she didn't have any use for banjo pickers. Yet she liked singing the gospel hymns in church."

Mama herself loved music and played the organ. She sang the old gospel songs of the Baptist church and the new Presbyterian songs taught by the Reverend Carl Higgins. After Carl left to become a foreign missionary, young Pastor Horne came to our Presbyterian church and taught some more new songs.

Pastor Horne preached about heaven for the believer in Christ. But he didn't dwell on the golden streets, the harps, and the pearly gates the way the Baptists did. He said he'd leave the colorful description of the supreme place in God's hands where it belonged. Just being wholly with God at last would be an eternal heaven, he declared.

In talking about heaven, Pastor Horne was very insistent on the necessary steps to get there, though. First, one had to repent of his sins and lean on the Lord for His forgiveness and love. That was only the

beginning. Believing James to be one of the
guidebooks in the Bible, Pastor Horne
couldn't abide faith without works and
a loving concern for others.

And Mama was like that, too. After her
public profession of faith and baptism, the
love in her heart for her neighbors just
naturally spilled over into their lives.
"After all, the more you love God, the more
you will love people, even though they
possess feet of clay," she said.

Mama admitted that she herself possessed
feet of clay, just as everyone else. They
were the only feet she owned to walk her
path to heaven. To her regret, every now
and then they led her astray from her goal
of sensing perfect communion with her
Creator and her dream of inhabiting
heaven someday.

"Whatever heaven's description, it is built
with love," Mama decided. She stopped to
look up at the June sky as blue as a baby's
eyes. "Heaven must surely be running over
with love for Christ, the real, perfect
Son of God."

She lifted her left eyebrow to weigh her
opinion. "Why, here on earth, love needs
an object," she said. "How can we possibly
love without loving individual persons for
who and what they are? Still, we must

admit that every once in a while we meet someone who is—or seems—unlovable."

Papa was sitting near the window reading about the life of Charles Spurgeon, the great preacher. "Now there was a man," he said, "a man with a capital **M**. Just think how many souls he saved. With the help of the Lord, of course."

"Of course," Mama said as she churned butter near the stove. "Will, Kate Rankin sets me all edgy at times. I can't ever be a Charles Spurgeon with his big soul."

Papa stopped reading to smile a slow smile.

"Will Jennings," Mama exclaimed, "just why do you have to look like that everytime I mention Kate's name? You can't forget that she once set her cap for you, I suppose."

"But she didn't get me. You did, Betsey. As you know, I never once went to see her."

Mama's blue eyes sparkled suddenly. She tucked a little brown curl into the bun on her neck. "I know, Will. And I shouldn't feel about Kate the way I do, of course. It's just that she gossips about everyone so. If only she'd learn that you can't raise your own height by lowering the reputation of the person near your elbow."

Papa's eyes twinkled. "Now, Betsey, you. . . ."

"Oh, Will!" Mama lifted her churn dasher to test the cream. "Sure, I gossip a wee bit, the same as everyone else. But nothing except general news. Kate, though, nibbles at people's reputations more often than she does her food."

"What's Kate dishing out now?"

"Will," Mama said slowly, "she thinks Stanton Trelawney must have killed someone. That's why he took moody spells at his brother's and why he left so suddenly, she thinks."

Papa looked down at his book, then stared at his left shoe but said nothing.

"I know how you feel about Stanton even yet. But for some reason, Will, I've had a certain feeling about him ever since we found my jelly in church that day."

Papa continued to stare at his shoe. He knew about Mama's "certain" feelings. More than once her intuitions proved to be substantial and very valid.

"Another thing about Kate. She's bragging around that she'll bring the best pie to the church social, and of course, her washing is always whiter than anyone else's," Mama added in a tart tone.

Without a word, Papa looked at the book

on Spurgeon, then scooted back into its lofty
pages, and Mama began to churn vigorously.

At the church social two days later, Kate
Rankin, a spry, little, fast-walking woman
with bright, brown sparrowlike eyes,
contributed three tasty-smelling strawberry
pies to the bountiful meal. Even Mama had
to admit they were delicious.

She had to admit something else, too,
before the day ended. The gray sky dripped
rainy tears and the creek had risen. While
the ladies were clearing the table, my
brothers and the other boys went outside
to play. Suddenly Mama heard a scream.
It was John's cry, she knew. She rushed
outside in terror. My second brother had
fallen into the creek.

"John, John!" she cried above the roar
of the brown waves rushing forward.

"Betsey!" Kate Rankin cried out just
behind her.

With no thought for her best clothes or
her beloved flowered dust cap that she
always wore, Kate leaped into the water.
She grabbed John's arm. Holding him fast,
she waded back to the bank.

"John, oh, John," Mama murmured,
hugging him close. "And, Kate, oh, thank
you Kate. You have a heart of gold," she
said warmly.

That night Mama prayed a long time on
her knees. Misunderstanding and ill-will
come from a lack of love and knowledge,
she decided. And walking the pathway to
heaven was all tied in with loving fellow
earthen vessels for themselves despite their
faults. Walking the path meant clinging
to God and faith amid daily trials and
vexations. It meant asking forgiveness for
wrong thoughts and actions and helping
one's neighbor when needed.

"Trivial matters can fence us from our
neighbors, Will," Mama observed the next
day. "But trouble makes kinfolk of us all.
I believe God has a hand in all events.
I believe He had a hand in what happened
yesterday."

Her calm sure voice held the firm quality
of the earth, our land. She and Papa sat by
the window, watching Clayton and John
play in our wide field.

"Belief is a wondrous word, Betsey," said
Papa. "If one doesn't believe in something,
his mind will wither and dry at the roots.
Without roots or a firm ground to stand on,
a person dies inwardly."

"Oh, Will, you have such a knack of
getting to the core of things!" Mama paused
in thought. "Kate Rankin is a person with
strong roots and a good heart—despite

everything. . . . Oh, John," she murmured, watching her second son chase blue butterflies.

"We all have feet of clay," she continued. "I stumble on mine all too often. Will they ever get me to heaven, I wonder?"

"All of us stumble on feet of clay, I guess," Papa replied.

Mama walked to her kitchen window to look up at the blue sunlit sky. She folded her tiny plump hands on the windowsill and smiled up at God.

"Will, how about a kettle of fresh vegetable soup?" she asked, turning to her worktable. "I'll take some to Kate and a bowl to Hannah Gettering."

Thinking of her neighbors and the friendships shared in Deep Valley, Mama continued her steps on her path to heaven.

# Mama Stands on Her Principles

"A day without a slice or two of solitude is like a cake without icing or a stream without water," Mama said one spring morning. "My soul grows parched and dry without a few moments to be still with God.

"In arranging my schedule," she declared, "I need to stop and map out my course to remind myself that an inward compass steered by the Lord guides my steps and values."

For half an hour that day, she sat arranging her values instead of the furniture. As she sorted her thoughts and shared them with the Lord, she seemed detached from her sprightly everyday self. Her being flowed in communion with Him as she attempted to see things whole. In the overall portrait she grasped for the "everythingness" in the life that she and Papa shared together.

Mama knew that refusing to let go
of the past and racing ahead to the future
narrowed the present road to a thin path.
Still, in that present moment she reviewed
the past as it had been shaped by Papa's
principles and her walking by his side.

Papa set great store by his principles,
which guided his beliefs and helped him
to stand firm on his opinions. Not for a
moment would he permit a favorite
principle to fall by the wayside.

In the years that Mama had been walking
by his side, the pair had shared many
worthwhile values: truth, love, and hope,
among many. Both practiced principles of
trust, a forgiving spirit, and perseverance.
And even though the journey proved
excessively hard at times, Mama tried to
follow the difficult principles of meekness
and patience in everyday problems.

"Only in the principle about our faith,
Lord," she said directly to her Maker, "lies
a difference that sometimes slices a thin
silence between us. Will is guided by his
steadfast principles, but my heart alone
guides my beliefs."

She reviewed the occasions when she
and Papa had attended the Primitive Baptist
Church. Papa had listened intently to the
sermons, but on the way home he proclaimed

that his opinions on faith could never run
parallel to those of some of the preachers.

"I believe in God, pray for forgiveness,
and trust Him daily with my life, Betsey,"
he'd told Mama more than once. "Yet I can't
go against my principles in joining a church
I don't believe in wholeheartedly."

That spring morning Mama sighed as her
blue eyes noted the hole in her ancient sofa.
Perhaps turning it away from the window
would make the hole less visible.

"Mending the holes in life is more difficult
than mending the furniture, Lord," she said
softly within her heart. "Dear Father, a small
hole edges around my heart because I've
never acknowledged You publicly in
church. Deep philosophical ideas or hard-to-
understand theology can never disturb my
comforting belief, though, even if Will does
let his principles keep us from joining the
church. I love You, dear Father, with my
whole heart—You know that. And I've
prayed for Your forgiveness and mercy
and feel that You have saved me. I'll keep
praying that You will work it out so that
Will and I can unite with the church."

Mama smiled as she looked out the
window toward the tall curving hills in
Deep Valley. The hills had beckoned her
ancestors into Kentucky and were ever

there, a fortress of strength; but her earth-bound eyes hadn't looked to them for some time. Today, on one of her "ginning" days she would make the time since her actions centered only where her heart led her. The mountain word describing ways of freedom with no set schedule had been handed down by her grandmother.

"I think I'll just gin around the house today," she had told Papa, my four brothers, and me that morning. "The rest of you just tend to yourselves for a change. I won't need your help. The Lord and I will be working alone today."

She had meant no irreverence to her Maker. She simply meant that she'd take time to talk to God and become reacquainted with her soul.

"After all," Mama said, "everyone inhabits two worlds—one reserved for his inner self, another shared with the world."

As she shared her inner self with God, Mama observed that spring was edging around the cornfield and lawn bathed in the lean March sun. She tucked a stray brown curl in the neat bun on her neck and saw Aunt Noreen entering the yard.

"Betsey, I've accepted the Lord and He's forgiven my sins!" Aunt Noreen confided a moment later. "I joined the church yesterday over in Lonesome Cove."

"You don't say!' declared Mama. "Did Ed make a fuss?"

Mama knew, as did everyone else, that Uncle Ed had no use for the church. The brother of a certain preacher had once cheated him out of a store debt. Since then he'd held the nonpayment of $2.81 against all churches, although the dishonest man belonged to only one.

"No, Ed didn't fume, not even a sentence. For some reason he has been different lately. I know he isn't well."

"He ought to see Doc Wainwright."

"Ed wouldn't hear of doctoring. He feels about doctors the way he does about preachers," sighed Aunt Noreen. "'No use for either of them,' he says. But—he's changed just lately. Why, for the first time he didn't complain about taking me to church yesterday."

"With the children taking turns at the measles for weeks, Will and I have been rather slack in our church attendance," Mama said with regret.

"Betsey, I can't explain how I feel inside, not even to myself. But God's miracles, I suppose, don't need words or noise."

"The silent things we feel inside are the real life," Mama mused.

"You see, Betsey, I did what I had long
wanted to do when I walked up and gave
the preacher my hand. I've prayed for
forgiveness and have turned to Christ at last.
I'll be baptized at the next baptism."

The weeks following Aunt Noreen's
conversion were filled with anticipation of
the baptism. "The meaning of my step in
faith grows deeper as the time draws near,"
Aunt Noreen confided to Mama. "Just think,
Betsey, this step is the first one I've ever
truly made on my own. In everything
else I've been guided by our parents, Ed,
or others."

The excitement over the baptism
increased twofold when we learned further
news. Hearing the announcement first,
Mama—for a wonder—kept it to herself
until she'd served the blackberry cobbler
at supper one night.

"You couldn't guess the news in twenty
years," she began, her blue eyes aimed
directly at Papa. "Ed accepted the Lord, too,
and will be baptized along with Noreen."

If Mama had announced that all the hills
in Deep Valley would be shaken by an
earthquake, we couldn't have been more
astounded! To think that Uncle Ed, who
never let an opportunity escape without
speaking cynically of the church, was

placing his name on the church roll book
was just too much for any of us to digest
immediately.

As he attended to his food, Papa's brown
eyes concentrated on his plate. Mama's
meaningful stare at Papa continued.

"Will. . . ." She turned to look at Clayton,
her eldest son. Her eyes turned toward my
brothers, John, Jim, and Jerry, and then to
me. "Jenny," she murmured, squeezing
my hand.

"The children, Will," she began bravely.
"We've brought them up to believe in God,
read the Bible to them, and prayed with
them. But we've never accepted the Lord
in public. As parents, shouldn't we? . . ."

Papa sprang from the table to his height
of six feet, three inches.

"I accept my Lord in public every day,
Betsey!" He snapped his sentence against
Mama's last syllable in the fastest speech
he'd ever made.

"I witness daily for Him by my actions
and work. And I'm for the church, Betsey,"
he declared positively, "for all churches,
despite my reservations on some of their
beliefs. If only you could understand once
and for all that I can't join a church until
I get a few things straightened out about its
members and doctrine! The action would

be wholly against my principles."

Seeing him so roused before us children, Mama hurriedly returned to her usual sprightly self. "Why, of course, Will, whatever you say."

A small plump figure less than five feet tall, she rose to stand sturdily by Papa's side. She smiled at the boys and me, but her smile seemed forced by merely a fraction.

"The chores," she reminded us. "Who's doing the milking tonight?"

The next morning Mama chatted and laughed cheerfully, ignoring Papa's explosion. Later on in the firefly twilight, Aunt Noreen's oldest son, Sam, brought the news. Uncle Ed had suddenly slumped over. A heart attack, Doc Wainwright had said.

"A heart attack!" Mama exclaimed in disbelief. "But no one in Deep Valley has ever had a heart attack!"

"I've read of heart disease," Papa said quietly.

"You've read of everything, Uncle Will. My father never read anything. Last week he said he was going to start reading the Bible. Now he won't have the chance." Sam's tears dripped from his wet eyelashes.

Mama and I were crying, too. "Just think,

Ed worked on the barn roof today," Mama murmured through her tears. "And he went—just like that."

I reached up to hold her arm tightly. So strange it was, this going-awayness called death. Grown-up people always spoke in wonder and awe of the farewell. No matter how often it came, people still marveled over how they'd seen someone a mere hour or perhaps a week before the person's soul had taken flight. Life was moving and talking and seeing. Death was all solid still like a frozen creek or cold December snow.

"Anyone can go—like that," Papa said quietly. "That is, with heart disease."

Uncle Ed was buried three days later, a week before the time planned for the baptism. At the funeral the preachers asked Aunt Noreen if she wished to postpone being baptized.

"No," she replied firmly. "I want to more than ever now, although it will be hard thinking what might have been. Ed beside me in the water—that would have been the happiest moment of my life."

On Sunday our family started for Lonesome Cove while the dewdrops still played hide-and-seek among the flowers. The morning, new as the Garden of Eden, was all filled with wonder and promise and

singing free of yesterday's used hours. A
sparkling sun splashed patterns of silvery-
shadowed lace among the tiny green leafy
ruffles trimming the trees. White trillium
blooms and dewy velvet violets crinkled
out and up, reaching toward the sun.

After the church service, people sang
as they walked down to the creek to a spot
filled with clear, gushing bubbles from
a slight waterfall. We stood under the
trees near mossy green rocks to watch
Aunt Noreen's baptism.

And then at the spot, the preachers who
were to dip Aunt Noreen into the water
began the old gospel song, "I Intend to
Go Through with Him."

The singing was what did it, Mama said
later. Not Aunt Noreen's decision, Uncle
Ed's death, or anyone else's influence.
When she'd thought of the meaning in the
words of the song, Mama knew she couldn't
wait another moment. She'd believed in God
all her life, read her Bible, and attempted to
witness daily for her Lord. But she suddenly
knew that wasn't enough.

Mama at last realized that she couldn't
hold back and expect others, even Papa,
to guide her heart in accepting Christ fully
in repentance and following Him in baptism.
As she sang softly by Papa's side, Mama

looked up at him. He continued singing
in vibrant tones. Her eyes shining with
determination, Mama slipped quietly from
his side. She started toward the preacher
holding the song book. Looking up at his
tall height, she placed her small hand
confidently in his.

Aunt Noreen and Mama were baptized
together that Sunday afternoon, while the
sun smiled through the trees and on the
mossy rocks and gurgling waterfall.

"I simply had to stand up for the love
in my heart, Will," Mama confided to Papa
that night. "Because, you see, this love I
have inside for Christ in knowing that He
died on the cross for me just grew so full
I couldn't do anything else."

"I'm glad for you, Betsey," Papa said
gently.

"If only Ed. . . ." Mama laid her hand
on Papa's.

Papa meditated while staring hard at
his left shoe.

"Death is a glorious sunrise for the
Christian," Mama said quietly. "Believing
in Christ's resurrection, I know that heaven
is as real as earth. No earthly event can
destroy my belief. If only you, Will. . . ."

The two remained silent several
moments.

But Mama couldn't remain serious long.
Her spirit had always been buoyant and
cheerful because of the inner joy and peace
her faith gave her. She couldn't abide the
role of a dour-faced, pessimistic Christian.

Now, after her public baptism, she
suddenly noticed something she had
overlooked. Her merry voice rang out across
the kitchen as she began to share it with
Papa.

"Will, it's truly a paradox, you know.
I kept trusting that if I loved God and placed
my life in His care, that should be enough.
At least, I hoped it might be. I didn't see
that principles mattered in faith, and I
resented the ideas you attached to yours.
You had no right, I thought, to let them
hinder us from joining the church."

She hesitated, looking toward Papa to
see if he followed her thought.

Mama then spoke the most positive
sentence she'd ever uttered in his presence.
"Today, although I didn't think of my action
as such, I stood on my own principles in
doing what I know is right for me, the
children, and, yes, for you, too, Will.
The tiny hole around my heart has
disappeared," she added softly.

Papa observed her set chin and her small
uplifted shoulders. His glance held a hint

of sadness intermingled with a thread of wistfulness. Yet standing tall by her, he asserted in tones as firm as hers, "I still can't join the church, Betsey."

"No one who loves his neighbor and reads the Bible as you do can be far from God," Mama declared. "He's just waiting for you to lift the latch from your heart and enter His door. Keep praying, Will."

She rose to stand by Papa. Together they watched the glowing fireflies beneath the gray-purple sky. In shared companionship they listened to the whippoorwill singing near the old well sweep.

"I love you, Will Jennings," Mama murmured softly. "Tonight more than ever."

# 🌸 Mama's Fifty Jelly Jars

The reason Papa couldn't join a church until he believed wholeheartedly in its doctrine revolved around his search for a perfect church. Since Mama was more practical and less idealistic than Papa, she knew he'd never attain his goal.

"Will," she reflected once, lifting her left eyebrow in thought, "why look for a perfect church containing perfect people? You'll never find it, since churches consist only of sinners saved by grace. Since you read your Bible so much, you must know that even its pages tell of men who made mistakes."

Papa held the Bible high in esteem. He never criticized God's Word. Instead, he let its holy principles correct him.

The Bible's holy principles, however, didn't keep Papa from speaking critically on the size of the preachers' minds in the Primitive Baptist Church, and the Old

Regular Baptist churches, the only churches
close enough for us to attend. Mama said
the size of their minds didn't count with
her. What counted was the brimming-over
measure of love and feeling when those
Spirit-filled men expounded the Scripture.

"Spirit or no," said Papa, "some preachers
ramble around for hours without feeding
the congregation even a spoonful of spiritual
food."

Also, he knew three preachers who were
dishonest and one who had a roving eye for
the ladies. It was hard for Papa to digest
such hypocrisy.

The church doctrine of predestination was
one he couldn't digest fully either. It didn't
tie in with his principle of believing in free
will and man's right to choose his own
path. Even the church members sometimes
argued over the meaning of predestination.
And when two ministers asserted that their
church held the only true deed to heaven,
Papa knew he'd never adjust his broad
steps to such narrow land.

He still continued attending church with
Mama, though. Then one day the Reverend
Floyd Delaney, a Presbyterian from a big
city up North in Ohio, began a Sunday
school and a church in Deep Valley. We
started going there.

One Sunday, Papa forgot about his

principles. He didn't stop to consider the
doctrine of the Baptists, the Presbyterians,
or any other church. Like Mama, he knew
at last that his love for Christ was so full
that he simply had to step forward at the
invitation. In that moment he realized that
he didn't need more ideals or principles.
Instead, he needed the Christ who had died
for his sins.

A few weeks later, Mama and Aunt
Noreen were both moved by the pastor's
sermon in the Presbyterian service. They
walked the aisle together and became
Presbyterians. Mama was so happy that she
and Papa were at last in accord on their
religious faith that she sang without ceasing
as she worked.

The Reverend Delaney had now returned
to Ohio, leaving young Carl Higgins to
preach and lead the Sunday school. Our
former pastor wrote that his church was
raising money to help start a new building.
And the Women's Missionary Union, after
hearing how their new pastor had enjoyed
Mama's apple jelly, wished to buy fifty jars.
They would pay fifty cents for each jar and
the cost for shipping them.

Mama was elated. "To think that the
minister liked my jelly so well that he told
others about it!"

All seven of us helped pack the jelly into

two boxes on the back porch. That night everyone talked about our treasure of twenty-five dollars. Mama said the money would belong to all of us since we'd all helped. Together we planned an order of new clothes and shoes from the catalog.

To our surprise, the next morning we found our ordering had been in vain. Mama's fifty jelly jars on the porch had disappeared!

"It just can't be!" Mama cried in disbelief.

Papa lifted his right hand to his chin in thought. The boys and I huddled together and counted our loss.

"I'd like to catch that thief!" Mama exclaimed heatedly. "To think that someone stooped low enough to steal my jelly!"

"Betsey," said Papa, "not one word spoken in anger will help the situation."

"I know Will. And I'll pray contritely tonight for losing my temper, of course. Right now, though, I'm sizzling with anger."

Mama did pray contritely that night. And Papa was right; not one angry word brought back the jelly. Neither did the words we used to tell the neighbors lead to any clue.

In the next few weeks Papa visited the neighbors to enlist help for our new church. Several men volunteered to cut timber and haul logs. Jonah Malone agreed to saw the lumber free.

Almost everyone offered to help with the new Presbyterian church. The exceptions were a few elderly Baptist church members, who said Papa should understand their position. They couldn't help start a new group different from their own denomination. There had never been anybody but old-time Baptists in the hills, they said. What was the world coming to, they wondered, when "furrin" denominations started "meachin'" in? Still, all Christians were going to the same heaven, they added, and they would fellowship with us.

Papa loved these honest and God-fearing hill people, many of them his own relatives, but he refused to be discouraged by them. He was so exhilarated over his success in enlisting the necessary labor that he wrote the Reverend Delaney that God was really unlocking the doors fast to complete the building.

And then as suddenly as God had worked among us, unforeseen events closed the doors. The biggest snow in years poured down during the last week of October. From then until the first of March, one falling snow clutched the heels of another.

With more coal used in the cold weather, the snow proved a blessing in one way for us, though. Early in January the towns-

people started driving out to the valley
for coal. Since Papa had opened a new coal
bank in the fall, he was able to sell several
loads and get money for the items we'd long
wanted from the catalog.

One snowy day Mama went down to visit
Jacob and Cynthia Trelawney. Cynthia's
arthritis was acting up again, and Stanton
Trelawney, Jacob's brother, had the flu.
Stanton, a traveling peddler, had stopped
for a visit in September. Mama went down
to help out at the Trelawneys almost
every day.

Late one afternoon Mama returned home,
crying as if her heart would break. "Oh,
Will, I've never been so hurt in my life!"
she lamented. "I was helping Cynthia tidy
Stanton's room, and when we finished she
asked me to read a Bible chapter. Oh, Will!"
Mama's tears flowed fast once more.

Papa could only stare in bewilderment.

"So I began reading the first psalm.
Stanton acted rather queer, I thought, when
I picked up the Bible. He stared out the
window while I read. But, Will, I never
dreamed he'd say what he did!"

She stopped to cry on Papa's sleeve.
"When I finished, Stanton's eyes narrowed
to slits and he spit his words, 'Please, will
you put that book away—and go?' Cynthia

followed me to the porch and said her
brother-in-law has always been reserved
and odd. They hadn't seen him for years
till he came this fall. She thinks some
misery is weighting him down."

"Betsey!" Papa's brown eyes flashed fire.
"I'm going to see that man. No one can talk
to you like that!"

"Oh, no, Will!" Mama cried in terror.
"You mustn't!"

"I'm going, Betsey. I'll permit nobody to
talk like that about the Book I live by or
to speak disrespectfully to my wife!" He
stomped out to the porch.

Mama followed Papa and managed to
restrain him. It hurt him mightily,though,
to give up his intention of seeking an
explanation from Stanton for his rude
behavior.

In our devotional hour that night, Papa
was the one who did extra praying. "It's
hard, dear Lord, to remember Your words
on forgiveness when troubling situations
arise. And I still feel guilty for not standing
up for Your Word and Betsey, but You
know Betsey. . . ."

Like Mama, Papa talked to God as though
He stood present by our hearth, caring and
interested in all episodes revolving around
the Jennings clan.

Thanks to prayer and self-control Papa didn't knock at the Trelawneys' door. This had been a difficult problem indeed—not being able to stand up for his principles. And all because of Jesus' teachings and Mama, of course.

"If only I could think of myself for once, Betsey," he said, "instead of you, others, and the guiding hand of God."

Mama smiled. "You wouldn't be Will Jennings then," she said.

She was the first to hear that Stanton Trelawney had packed his clothes one Saturday and had left his brother's house. For the first time in months she breathed a sigh of relief.

Finally, after a long cold winter, spring tiptoed tentatively into the valley—and the long delayed work on the Presbyterian church began once more. Papa was so happy seeing the building grow that he forgot his earlier vexations. The church members in Ohio sent money for windows, a door, paint, and a heating stove. They also paid for the first order of Sunday school literature.

On a dewy May morning the church stood completed at last. It was a lovely, tall white building, beckoning against the hillside and dedicated to spread God's Word.

Together Papa and Mama, my brothers and I rode down in our buggy to see it.

"I can't believe it!" Mama exclaimed joyously. We could hear the smile in her voice. "I simply can't believe our church is completed at last."

We knew the building was real, for by this time we had entered it and were walking up the aisle to the pulpit. Near the front were two things we found extremely difficult to comprehend: two pasteboard boxes, the identical ones we'd packed months ago. When we opened them, we found they still contained Mama's fifty jars of jelly!

Mama looked down and discovered a paper with these words: "Here is your jelly, Mrs. Jennings. So just possibly I'm no thief after all. Yet no man acting as I did deserves forgiveness. Still, I prayed here last night. Stanton T."

"I can't see why he returned the jelly here in the church. Why didn't he return it to our back porch?" Mama wondered.

She lifted her left eyebrow in thought. "A person can be influenced mightily in a building dedicated to God," she observed.

None of us could know then how much Mr. Trelawney had been influenced as he had observed our labor for the church. Not until years later, when he finally placed the whole vexing problem of his life in God's care, did we know that he would pay tribute to Mama also.

"This building helped change my life," Stanton Trelawney would testify on that future date. "And then there was Mrs. Jennings' jelly that almost turned me into a thief. She turned my thought to repentance, though, when she came to my brother's house and read in Psalm 1 how the ungodly perish. I tried running from myself, even after that, but her words, along with God's, followed me through everything."

# 🌺 Miss Effie's Christmas Tree

Unlike Papa, who had acquired a high
school and a college degree, Mama didn't
continue her education beyond the eighth
grade in Deep Valley's little country school.
Yet she loved to read and read whenever
she had time to spare. Papa was proud of
her and said she had educated herself to
equal many with a college degree, except
perhaps for those in the scientific fields.

Mama herself admitted that she didn't
know a thing about science. The only
reasoning she knew was all bound up in
her love for God and people and in the
many pithy sayings and homespun wisdom
of her Scotch-Irish people and ancestors
from Old England who had journeyed into
the Kentucky hills in the early days. Mama
never forgot the old sayings or adages
handed down in her family. They were as
much a part of her life as eating, sleeping,

or praying daily. And Mama just simply wouldn't be Mama without them, we all agreed!

When Miss Effie came into Deep Valley to teach the school during the Depression years, she boarded at different homes. She stayed most often at our home. She and Mama read and discussed books together. They also shared the problems in the school. If a child needed a warm sweater or mittens, Miss Effie would tell Mama. Within a week Mama would have the items knitted, even if she had to unravel some of her great-aunt's legacy of knitted possessions—which she often did.

One Wednesday night in December, Mama sat knitting a sweater for little John Newcomb. The yarn had been unraveled from an ancient blanket unearthed from Aunt Sarah's trunk. While Mama knitted, Miss Effie read a biography, and then the two talked about Christmas, giving, and love.

"Give a spoonful of love and you'll be paid a cupful brimming over," Mama said, quoting from her Great-aunt Sarah's wisdom.

The next morning fresh snow covered our valley, making the pine trees on the hills look like Christmas trees. When Miss Effie, my brothers, and I walked to school, we

noticed that Mike Riley had gotten a roaring
fire going in the schoolhouse stove. He
stood waiting for us outside the door.

"Somebody's done stole your Christmas
tree!" he cried desperately, running across
the snow.

"Oh, no!" Miss Effie said, her toast-brown
eyes filled with disbelief.

"Oh, no!" the boys and I echoed just
behind her.

At first I thought Mike was just practicing
the special line he had in the Christmas
play, the sentence in which he substituted
"your tree" for "our tree" despite Miss Effie's
daily correction. But when we entered the
room that gray December morning and
observed the glow from the old Ben
Franklin stove light up the bare corner
where the tree had stood, we realized
indeed that the tree was gone.

"Miss Effie's tree," we continued calling it,
although our teacher repeatedly reminded
us that it was "our tree" since it belonged to
all of us, her twenty-six pupils. But we
knew better—Mike Riley, the boys and I,
the Lindsay twins, Billy Newcomb, Jane
Epling, and the other scholars. We knew
better because in all of Deep Valley no one,
until Miss Effie had come along, had ever
owned a Christmas tree.

For all of us, Christmas meant hanging up

our black stockings on Christmas Eve. And finding them on Christmas morning filled with peppermint candy, an orange or two, perhaps a rag doll, or a small drum and wooden toys carved by our fathers. Christmas in my family meant hearing Papa read the Christmas story from the Bible. It meant planning ahead for suspense-filled weeks and attending church for the special program on Christmas Eve. But Christmas had never meant a Christmas tree until that snowy sunlit day when Miss Effie had sent Mike Riley and my brother Jim to the woods for a fresh green cedar.

Every afternoon after that, we'd finish our lessons early, then practice the Christmas play and make lovely decorations for the tree. We covered hickory nuts with pictures cut from catalogs, pasted little handles to the nuts, and hung them up as bells. From colored paper we cut thin strips, made them into chain links which we joined to form long garlands for our Christmas tree.

The Lindsay twins and I had made stars, Mike had brought popcorn to string, and everyone had drawn pictures of candles and angels. Jane Epling had drawn the picture of the Christ Child. To us, Miss Effie's Christmas tree was the loveliest in the world.

Every afternoon as we left school, we would gaze fondly but regretfully at the Christmas tree. In bright anticipation each morning we would hurry back to school to enjoy it anew. But now that shining chapter of our lives had ended. Miss Effie's tree had disappeared.

It was hard for us to concentrate on lessons that morning. Instead, we kept eyeing the broken windowpane, covered with cardboard since early October. Hard as it was to believe, someone had evidently entered through that pane, picked up the tree, and then departed through the larger window nearby since it was found unlocked. The culprit had been so careful that not a single chain link, bell, or other decoration had fallen to the floor.

Outside, on the playground a zigzagging wind swished the snow about in little twirls. The bigger boys ventured out to play, but most of us remained in the schoolroom at recess, listening to Miss Effie read stories. For the first time, however, we failed to give our wholehearted attention.

All any of us could think about was the missing Christmas tree and how desolate the schoolroom had grown without it—the way Mary and Joseph must have felt when no one welcomed them to the inn. How could

we possibly continue our play, invite our
parents in, and not have the beautiful tree
to display as we'd planned?

"We'll practice as usual," Miss Effie
informed us that afternoon, standing erect
and tall like the poplar trees in our old
North Hollow.

"But the tree!" Mike Riley exclaimed.
"We can't have the play without your
Christmas tree!"

"We'll practice as usual," Miss Effie
repeated. "Afterward," she added, lowering
her voice in the manner she used to assure
undivided attention, "you, Mike, and Jim
may go for another tree."

"Another tree!" Mike Riley cried, feeling
so amazed he almost dropped his slate.

"Oh, Miss Effie!" Lena Lindsay squealed.

"But we don't have time to make new
decorations!" wailed Lila, her twin.

"We'll make the time," Miss Effie
affirmed. "We'll do what we can here, then
work at home tonight."

So, that afternoon we practiced as usual,
except that Jim had to take Billy Newcomb's
part since Billy was absent. His little brother
was sick. Billy thought heaps of his small
brother, we knew. Little John was just about
all the family Billy had—little five-year-old
John for whom Mama was knitting the
sweater.

"What if Billy isn't here tomorrow?" Lena asked, as we worked on the decorations after play practice.

"It must be dreadful not to have a mother," Jane Epling reflected. Mrs. Newcomb had died the spring before, leaving her husband and the two boys.

Outside, snow skeins unraveled from a bleak, gray sky while we made bells, garlands, stars, and pictures.

Lila broke the silence, wondering aloud in frustration: "I just don't see who stole the Christmas tree!"

"Perhaps someone needed it more than we do," Miss Effie commented thoughtfully.

"More than we do!" Lila exclaimed in exasperation.

The rest of us nodded in unanimous assent. No one could possibly need a Christmas tree more than we did right there in the schoolroom for the Christmas play!

Everyone glanced at the empty corner. And at that moment a thought resembling one of Mama's "certain" feelings hit me like the sudden ringing of a bell.

"I don't believe anyone would really steal a Christmas tree—despite the story in our Christmas play," I said slowly. "Why, that would be like stealing from a church."

All eyes turned toward me. I hesitated in shy uncertainty and shook my pigtails in embarrassment. But Miss Effie encouraged me with her special "go ahead" smile, and I proceeded falteringly. "The tree with its wonder and beauty stands for love and the spirit of giving. So, nobody could possibly steal a Christmas tree. People don't need to steal God's love because, Mama says, He gives it to us every day."

"But who took the tree then?" Lila asked. "If it wasn't stolen," she added grudgingly.

By that time the boys had returned, and everyone began rushing about, getting in one another's way. Singing carols while we trimmed the second tree, we failed to hear the steps outside. Only when the door opened did we look around to see Billy Newcomb standing just inside the doorway with Miss Effie's Christmas tree!

"Miss Effie. . . ." Billy's voice faltered. Then taking a step forward, he said, "I'm—sorry—but I borrowed your Christmas tree. For little John."

"Why, Billy," said Miss Effie, holding a chain in mid-air as she started toward him.

"I borrowed your tree," Billy continued more bravely, "because I needed it real bad—for John."

"John?" Miss Effie asked apprehensively.

"He's better now," Billy assured her. "But he was real sick last night. You see, Pa was on the night shift in the mines, and I got scared John was going to die."

Near the second Christmas tree, each of us remained rooted to our respective places, all ears alert to Billy's words.

"I wanted to bring him down here for the play tomorrow," Billy continued, "but when he got sick, I was afraid he might die without seeing your Christmas tree, Miss Effie. He's better now, so I brought back your tree," he finished quietly, his voice dropping softly like the snow beyond the windowpanes.

Billy walked toward Miss Effie's desk and carefully set the tree down. "Miss Effie," he said softly, looking small indeed near her tall form. "I didn't really steal your tree, did I? I just borrowed it for a while—for John, because he's my little brother."

Miss Effie laid a gentle hand on Billy's shoulder and smiled at him. Then she turned to smile at all of us, her love radiant and warm.

"No, you didn't steal the tree, Billy. When you took it to share with John, you were sharing love," she explained kindly. "So you weren't stealing at all. Because love is for giving, you know, not stealing. And only by giving it away can we keep it for ourselves."

Miss Effie turned to include the rest of us in her explanation. "And that holds true for

Christmas trees, God's love, all loveliness,
and the Christmas spirit—when all take part
in creating the faith and hope behind things
like these." Her voice, as always, stopped
on just the right note.

"Billy," she continued, "you take that tree
straight back to little John. He'll be needing
it for Christmas Eve."

"Your Christmas tree!" Billy exclaimed.

"John's Christmas tree," Miss Effie
corrected firmly. "And yours," she
added more softly. "I need no tree for
myself alone."

The next April, Mr. Newcomb was killed
in the mines, and Billy and little John were
left alone. Mama couldn't wait to send Papa
after them. The boys stayed with us a year
until an aunt from Indiana took them in.

In the year that the Newcomb boys
stayed with us, Mama helped them with
their lessons and read to them. Years later
when the brothers graduated from college,
they each sent her a lovely card of
appreciation and a letter telling how
much she'd helped them.

"Give a spoonful of love and you'll be
paid a cupful brimming over!" Mama
exclaimed when she received Billy's letter.
Then she recalled the episode of Miss Effie's
Christmas tree from years before: "Miss Effie

said love is for giving, and only by giving it away do we keep it for ourselves. How right she was! Christmas trees and love for people and for God are for sharing always with others."

## 🌸 Mama and Hannah Gettering

Although Hannah Gettering and Mama were both alike in many ways, Mama didn't seem to be aware of the similarities.

"Hannah is just so different from anyone else," she decided one summer afternoon, while the thirsty robins beyond our doorway sang loudly for rain.

As Mama stirred cornmeal mush on the stove, I thought about the tall elderly lady who had moved into the little whitewashed house up the hollow down past the crossroads a few months before.

Papa sat mending a harness in the little lean-to room off the kitchen. Suddenly he stopped to look out the window toward our parched garden near the dry grass and then returned to work with no comment.

Mama, adept at carrying on a one-sided conversation, however, continued her thought. "Hannah's difference lies in the fact that she doesn't consider herself a visitor on earth."

Papa held a tack in the air to examine it carefully.

As Mama tested the mush, she enlightened him further. "No, Hannah isn't stopping as company on this earth for a mere while, looking to be served the way some folks are. Like Dan Bender, for instance," she added tartly, as she stirred the mush vigorously and thought of the laziest man in our valley.

She reached for a bowl. "Dan expects to find life ready-made in a surprise package. If only he'd use his muscles to mold it from minutes and hours!"

A twinkle appeared in Papa's eyes as he examined another tack.

"Now, Will. . . ." Mama halted just like Blarney, our mule, when Papa itched to finish plowing before rain soaked the newly tilled ground.

Papa's eyes twinkled as if he were preparing to tease her about gossiping. She stirred the mush energetically again, but her mouth remained as tightly closed as our stuck dresser drawers in summer months.

Not until that evening when we sat on our back porch in the summer moonlight did Mama resume her subject.

"What I meant, Will," she began slowly, testing her words, "is that Hannah is not a visitor on earth because she stands tall each day to inhabit it as a dedicated permanent tenant while she continues her earthly life. And I guess some of us don't."

At the slight emphasis of the "us" uttered in Mama's repentant voice, Papa laid his rough hand on her soft brown hair. He smoothed my brown pigtails and took me on his lap.

"No, I suppose not," he agreed. "Most of us aren't grateful enough for the time God provides. We let many days slide by without making them count."

"But not Hannah!" Mama asserted happily, her spirit climbing because she and Papa were now sharing similar thoughts. "Just by little things, Hannah Gettering shows that she believes the Lord wants all days to count."

"Like gifts meant to be used, rather than ones stored on a shelf."

"Yes." Mama savored the moment, tasting the meaning in their congenial thoughts. "Will," she said then, "Hannah uses at least three-fourths of her days for other people. She certainly doesn't hoard time for herself."

I remembered the time Aunt Hannah had rocked me when I had had the croup, and

the day she had cleaned our house and
cooked supper when Mama was sick.

Just before we left the refreshing night
air and went inside, Mama made a final
statement. "Life can be either a stumbling
block or a stepping-stone," she reflected.
"To Hannah, every event is a stepping-stone
leading to a higher step in faith."

The next day was hot and humid. As the
dry weather continued, our grass grew more
crisp and brown. Our bean vines and
cornstalks shriveled. Several wells dried
up in Deep Valley. As the neighbors carried
water from the deeper wells, they stopped
to comment on the record-breaking
dry spell.

The day that the weeping rain clouds
eventually appeared, John Tibbs, a half-
brother to lazy Dan Bender, came down with
typhoid. Everyone, except Aunt Hannah,
Mama and Papa, Sarah Ezelle, and
Mamie Malone, was afraid to cross his
threshold. The five took turns nursing John
and his wife, who had also contracted the
disease. Despite their combined effort,
Mr. and Mrs. Tibbs died, leaving their son,
Johnny, an orphan.

What to do with Johnny then became just
about the sole topic among us. Both sets of
grandparents were dead, and the other

relatives showed no desire to provide a home for the son of John Tibbs. Like his half-brother, Dan, John had also been idle and a heavy drinker.

"The kinfolk are afraid he'll take after his dad," Papa reflected.

Mama lifted her left eyebrow in thought. "Um." She looked out the kitchen window to observe the road where John Tibbs had often reeled by.

That afternoon Papa came home with the latest news. "Johnny has found a home. Hannah Gettering has taken him in," he disclosed.

"At her age!" Mama exclaimed. "She'll have a hard furrow to hoe."

As time passed, the prophecy proved true. Aunt Hannah took in laundry and peddled produce from the farm to increase her dollars. Mama often assisted her in gathering the vegetables for peddling and helped her make quilts to sell.

"Seed alone won't make a crop. Turning the soil and bending the back are necessary," Mama told us. "And Hannah needs help, if anyone does."

Not once, however, did Aunt Hannah complain. One day when Kate Rankin dished out an extra helping of sympathy, she replied in a matter-of-fact tone, "There's

no place to get off the route one takes
except at the end. Looking toward the goal
makes the traveling and scenery worthwhile.
Moreover, God never permits any problem
that He and I can't unravel together."

One afternoon in early spring Mama went
down to care for Aunt Hannah, who was
suffering from a deep chest cold. When
Mama prepared to return home, Aunt Hannah
motioned a thin hand toward the Bible. "Will
you read Psalm 46, Betsey?" she asked.

Mama quickly reached for the Holy Book
and turned to the psalm. "God is our refuge
and strength, a very present help in
trouble," she began.

A radiant glow of peace lighted the sick
woman's face.

Mama read the tenth verse: "Be still,
and know that I am God: I will be exalted
among the heathen, I will be exalted in
the earth."

Aunt Hannah turned to lay a gentle hand
on Mama's.

"The room was so silent I could almost
hear the grass grow round the lilac near the
windowpane," Mama told us later. "God's
presence showered right down on her bed
when she prayed aloud after I finished
reading. Before I left, she asked me to take
a glass of jelly to Grandma Simms."

"The way one acts while suffering brings out the type of person he is inside," Papa commented slowly. "And sharing desserts should be a treat for every Christian. Hidden ice cream only melts, of course."

"Hannah is always full of hope and thoughtful care," added Mama. "She thinks of others even amid her own pain. I guess her Bible reading helps her over the rough spots. She reads her Bible and spends more time in prayer on her knees than anyone in the valley, I believe."

Everybody knew Aunt Hannah read her Bible to Johnny and held a family devotion each night. So when he began running with bad companions in town, the whole neighborhood was stunned. Almost everyone expressed sympathy for Aunt Hannah. Only a few, remembering Johnny's father, exchanged the remark, "I told you so."

Hannah's faith in the boy, however, didn't waver a second. "There's still good in him," she asserted. "He needs my prayers now more than ever."

So, Aunt Hannah continued to pray even when Johnny ran away from home and the months crept by with no word from him. The spicy air of late September passed, October frost embraced the fallen leaves, and the November sky grew heavy with snow. Still, no word from Johnny.

Bright Christmas hope and its near fulfillment then spread across our snow-trimmed hills. Two days before Christmas, Mama visited Aunt Hannah.

"Trouble may be a dark mine, but men find rewarding metal in mines," Aunt Hannah told her. "With the help of the Lord my faith is strengthened each day—and my boy will come home."

"Why, of course," Mama answered firmly. "He may come as a Christmas present, you know."

But Christmas came and went, wet snow plastered the sleeping earth beside the hemlock trees, and still no word from Aunt Hannah's son.

January then passed with zero temperatures, February's brief days stumbled slowly from the calendar, and March, as usual, couldn't make up her mind to go or stay. At last, though, time opened the door for April, and a note of spring sang through the daylight hours. Deep Valley lay trimmed in green and gold. Crocuses bloomed and the hillside burst forth in virgin mint green after the bloom of bright redbud and nipped dogwood. And Johnny came home on that most glorious of all bright new beginnings—Easter morning, when the valley dawn shone as blue as the first dawn in Eden.

Aunt Hannah's prayers and those of Mama, who had been praying with her, were answered a hundredfold. The Johnny who had returned was not the old Johnny. In his place walked a tall, upright young man with a clean, trusting look on his face. He related his story to his foster mother just as the Easter sun cleared the mist from the mountaintop.

When he had left home, he wandered from one town to another spending his money on drink. One night on a misty, damp street he observed a Salvation Army meeting and heard, as he had often heard from Aunt Hannah, the story of Christ's love. As he listened, the taut string that had long been tied around his heart snapped asunder. With that severing, God's love enveloped him and tears of repentance flowed down his cheeks.

Now he was planning to return to school. He also intended to become a Salvation Army officer someday and tell others about the love of the Lord.

In matters of religious faith, Aunt Hannah was a dipped-under-in-the-water Baptist. She didn't know about General William Booth or the work of the Salvation Army on behalf of people in the big cities beyond our small community.

"Be that as it may, son," she said, "I'll fellowship with them since they have saved you. After all, the total light doesn't shine through a single window."

She couldn't wait to tell Mama the news.

That afternoon our family sat talking of the wondrous event. When Mama declared that Aunt Hannah's goodness and example in daily living had helped lay the groundwork for Johnny's conversion, I suddenly recalled the conversation of my parents on a summer moonlit night—the time when Mama had said that Aunt Hannah stood tall as a permanent tenant on earth. She'd said something, too, about stumbling blocks and stepping-stones.

I looked at Mama, who seemed to read my thoughts.

"Life," she said, as if continuing where she'd left off from that summer conversation, "can be either a stepping-stone or a stumbling block. It can be used as a ladder to climb to greater heights or as a broken stile that blocks one's pathway."

She stopped to observe the rays of Easter sunlight and then continued. "If we search for the good about us, the trials that will

surely crop up won't shrivel our faith and
trust. Hannah didn't allow the problem of
Johnny Tibbs to become a stumbling block
in her life. Instead, she saw his need and
used it to climb to further stepping-stones of
hope and faith. And I still say she was able
to succeed only because she reads her Bible
so much and prays diligently."

From his tall height Papa looked down
at Mama, who sat with our Bible in her lap.
He smiled tenderly and placed a gentle
hand on her shoulder.

"I always said Hannah was different from
other people," Mama said.

"All other people?" Papa asked, looking
intently at her.

I guess he was thinking, as I was, that
Hannah Gettering wasn't too different from
Mama. The pair resembled each other in
more ways than one.

# 🌺 Mama's Green Thumb

Mama, her cousin Mamie Malone, and
Hannah Gettering ran here and there doing
little things for others in Deep Valley. "Their
kitchens aren't big enough to keep them
busy," Papa teased one day. "So they
just naturally stir their fingers in the
lives of others."

He stopped smiling and then spoke
seriously. "Betsey, the three of you help
many people, of course. While performing
little acts of kindness for people, you often
leave behind a Christian principle that helps
a family straighten out their relationship to
each other and God."

On a bright April morning when the dew
and spider webs trailed powder puffs
diamond lattices on our lawn, Mama smiled
a special communion smile to God. Life
with nature was a prayer to her. She knelt
and with skillful fingers sifted and smoothed

the earth, preparing it for seed. She worked
in the same careful, loving manner that she
blended ingredients when making a pie.

"I love to sow my red salvia seed," she
declared. "We read of God's plan for
beautiful growth and necessities in Genesis.
In growing beauty, one reaches the heart
of creation and catches a glimpse of
the eternal."

"Your mama certainly has a green
thumb," Papa told my brothers and me
as he smiled a rare smile.

Clayton and John stood ready to help
him plow the garden, while Jim and Jerry
trimmed the grass near the fence. Near
Mama's side, I helped her prepare the soil
for her flower seed.

Our work was interrupted when Jacob
Trelawney came running to the gate. "We've
had a mine explosion!" he cried. "Elijah
Henson is hurt and we need help."

Papa and Clayton hurried down the road.
They helped take Elijah from the mine and
got him to the hospital where they waited.
When they returned home, we learned that
Elijah Henson had lost his eyesight.

I thought of the big giant of a man whom
Mamie Malone had led from the creek one
day after his wagon had fallen into the
water; she had later dished out the Scripture

to him. I remembered his footsteps heavy
across the planks of the old church barn
over in Lonesome Cove, as he ambled up
to give the preacher his hand. His wife, Lisa,
had since died, and he was now bringing
up their twelve-year-old twins by himself.

"It's strange to think that Elijah will
never be able to see again," Mama sighed
as she looked out the window at her
new flower bed.

Papa surveyed the fresh spring earth and
the late sun trailing farewell beams across
the meadow. Both remained silent as the
sun slanted on the lilac bush before scooting
over the rim of the hill.

April passed quickly and May
flowers trimmed the hillside. In late May,
Mr. Henson was able to return home. Papa
visited often to help him pass the time of
day. And Mama, Mamie Malone, and others
dropped in to clean and cook meals. After
a while, though, Elijah and the boys were
able to manage alone. In spite of his
blindness Elijah remained as independent
as ever.

"Will, I'm troubled a mite," Mama
remarked one day, watching bright sunlight
spread patterns across the lawn.

"You're concerned about Elijah," Papa
surmised, staring hard at his left shoe.

"Who wouldn't be troubled about Elijah Henson these days?" Mama demanded. "Actually, he has needed a helping hand for years now, with no one to do for him since Lisa died."

"One thing you can say for Elijah since he accepted the Lord," Papa reflected, "is that he's able to stand alone and doesn't permit bitterness to wound his soul despite his misfortune. His faith and trust in God have grown since he walked the barn floor that November day. He stands more courageously than ever in his blindness. It's as though he has suffered so much that he can face any situation without fear or help from anyone. Still, he doesn't have to live as if he is screwed into a hollow log."

"Um," said Mama, lifting her left eyebrow as she weighed her thoughts. She started to hoe her flowers. "I'd appreciate your help with the hoeing," she invited. Then continuing her work, she said, "It is one thing to stand alone. But there's something missing in the picture, Will, when a person has nobody with whom to share the labor and beauty of life. Elijah still misses Lisa very much."

She looked up at Papa to savor their companionship together.

He smiled down at her and pointed to the

first red bloom of the salvia. Mama turned
to look at it, then grew thoughtful once more.

"Oh, Will, I almost forgot that Elijah will
never be able to see beauty again! He's
learned to feel his way around so well that
I often forget he's blind."

Papa failed to reply, so Mama divulged
a thought she'd been sifting for days.

"Will. . . ." She leaned on her hoe.
"Somehow I have a certain feeling that
Melanie Bender has been interested in
Elijah for some time. And she still is,
I'd say, despite his blindness."

Papa chuckled softly. "You women," he
teased. "Better stick to growing flowers with
your green thumb instead of attempting a
love match, Betsey. If there's love between
the two, it will grow without your help."

"Um," Mama said as if to herself,
while observing the flowers she'd
prodded to maturity.

That summer she sowed a new bed of
phlox, kept an eye on her chrysanthemums,
and continued reading Genesis. She and
Melanie Bender visited each other
frequently. They'd been close friends since
Melanie's husband had been killed in a
mine accident and Mama had made a
Sunday bonnet for her and dresses for
the little girls.

Now they traded dress patterns, quilted,
and shared canning days together. Both felt
that life was framed in the everyday chores
of home life. After all, they agreed, one had
to frame life in some meaningful way.

They also agreed that God had acted
wisely in planting an instinct for domesticity
in women. While Mama observed her
friend's knack with household duties,
she thought of Elijah's need, and her
fingers itched to prod him out of his
male independence.

One autumn day she stood in her garden.
Hannah Gettering dropped in for a visit and
Mama gave her flowers. Danny and David
Henson passed by and she gave them some.
When Pastor Horne called that evening,
she also shared with him the beauty from
her garden.

The splendor of the flowers must have
impressed the pastor, because the next
Sunday he wove his sermon on the growth
of Christian character around the unfolding
stages of flowers. Outside the church door,
Elijah Henson told the pastor that he had
enjoyed growing flowers as a boy before
he'd started working in the mines.

I was so surprised to think that such a
strange old fellow as Elijah Henson could
possibly enjoy flowers that I almost dropped

my Bible! Looking at Mama, I saw that she, too, was astonished. She didn't allow her surprise to overwhelm her, however.

"You used to grow flowers?" she asked Elijah warmly, elated to find someone else interested in making God's world beautiful.

He turned to her. "I once dreamed of owning a greenhouse," he said quietly.

"I like flowers, too," Melanie Bender confided, as she stood by Mama. "Yet I can never grow them as Betsey does in her blossom patch."

A speculative gleam suddenly leaped into Mama's eyes. "I'll need help in gathering and labeling my seed this fall. Could you help me, Melanie? We could save seed for you to sow in the spring, Elijah," she offered.

"I take nothing without giving help in return," he answered determinedly. "So I'll help you and Melanie with the seed. I can tell the different kinds by feeling them."

The next June, Melanie Bender and Elijah Henson were married in the new flower garden in back of the Henson kitchen. The bride and the groom had tended it together. They now made plans to start a nursery to sell flowers and plants in town.

"Oh, Will," Mama exclaimed, "their marriage will succeed, I know, since they'll now work and enjoy life together."

She stopped to observe Melanie and Elijah among the flowers along with his sons, David and Danny, and the four Bender girls. "The family picture is complete at last," Mama said. "It's just as God intended, according to Genesis."

Papa chuckled softly. "Betsey, you certainly have a green thumb. In more ways than one."

"Why, Will," Mama retorted blithely, "helping human relationships to grow is even more important than growing flowers."

## 🎟 The Deacon Who Dropped the Collection Plate

Before Papa joined the church, he'd had a few slight disagreements with the neighbors. He and Charlie Lennon had quarreled over the building of a bridge near Charlie's property. Once, along with almost everyone else in the valley, Papa had taken a decided stand on a particular school issue. A lot of ruffled feelings emerged at high temperatures before time and common sense produced a cooler environment.

After becoming a staunch church member, though, Papa felt that maybe his differences with others were finished.

"Oh, no, Will," Mama said wisely. "You miss the point of Christianity in seeking for all **A** pluses on your report card. Be satisfied with a few **B's,** since no situation or human being ever reaches perfection. We'll have differences of opinion and slight tiffs even though we're walking the path to heaven."

The tiff that flared up between Papa and a fellow deacon occurred after Papa had become a real born-again Christian.

After Uncle Ed died of his heart attack, Ben Trainer, who owned a store in town, started riding out to Deep Valley. He came to advise Aunt Noreen on running the store Uncle Ed had left.

"It's the talk of the valley that Ben's store is closed two days a week," Mama told Papa.

She bit her sewing thread as Papa broke out into a rare smile. "Oh, Will, I can't help but listen to talk of my own sister."

"It's really Ben's business, isn't it, if he doesn't mind losing money?"

"Men!" fumed Mama. "Will, I don't care one pinhead what people say about his losing trade. What bothers me is the talk about Ed's being dead such a short time and now Noreen. . . ."

"Maybe your sister grows frustrated over caring for nine children, running a store, and managing a farm all at the same time."

"How she does all three is beyond me," Mama reflected. "Why, if I were left without you, Will. . . ."

Her tinkling laughter rang across the porch as she realized that Papa had caught her in a snare of words.

She threaded her needle in concentration. "Still, Noreen could wait a mite longer despite the work."

"She would really get a good husband if she captured a fine bachelor like Ben," Papa admitted.

"If she captured Ben! Why, have you forgotten that he used to be sweet on her when they were young? She turned him down for Ed. He left for the West after her wedding and didn't return for years."

"Ben never would talk about the West after he returned to the old Trainer place," Papa said. "He kept those years fenced tight as barbed wire to himself."

"He sure has a surplus of talk to share with Noreen now," Mama added.

Mr. Trainer continued to talk to Aunt Noreen. Yet no marriage took place between the two, even when he hired a manager for his store and moved back to the old homestead just down the road from us. Why he and Aunt Noreen didn't get married now that Uncle Ed had been dead a sufficient lapse of time to satisfy everyone, nobody seemed to know. Not even Mama, who had always been close to her sister. Everyone itched to learn the reason for the interrupted courtship.

Then one Sunday an event occurred that

turned talk in another direction. While Ben
Trainer and Papa were carrying the
collection plates down the church aisle, Ben
suddenly grew nervous and dropped his
plate on Jacob Trelawney's head. The silver
rolled all over and the few bills fluttered
down. Everyone was embarrassed beyond
speech, even if conversation had been
appropriate. Later, outside the church the
spectators of the unbelievable episode
shared opinions about why Ben had
dropped the plate in such nervous haste.

The next day Papa and Ben Trainer rode
into town to check on Ben's store. A man
and a young dark-eyed boy left the store as
the other two entered. Papa was surprised
to observe the man's shifty eyes beam a
hint of hatred directly at Ben.

On their way home together, Ben
remained aloof. Papa recalled that the man
and the boy had left abruptly. He also
remembered that pointed glance of hatred.
Something else stirred his thoughts. It
seemed as if he'd seen the dark-eyed boy
somewhere.

What troubled Papa more than anything
else, though, was the change in his friend
Ben. His shoulders slumped, he appeared
nervous, he spoke falteringly, and his eyes
held a lost, bewildered look.

On a sudden impulse Papa halted his horse. "Ben," he began carefully, "something is troubling you. I'd like to help if I can. Now if that man and boy. . . ."

Papa couldn't believe his ears as Ben's words hit the air in tight tones like ice chunks: "Nobody can help me! Mind your own business, Will, except for this. Tell Pastor Horne to look for another deacon!"

Papa was so hurt he couldn't sleep that night. To think that he had only been trying to help when Ben had flared up so vehemently, but it was the wounded look in Ben's eyes that continued to haunt him.

On Wednesday, Papa went down to the Trainer farm. As he neared the gate, Ben came down the path along with the man and the boy who had been in the store. Staring hard at the boy, Papa suddenly knew who he was.

When the pair once more left in a hurry, Papa approached his friend. "I just had to try again with you, Ben," he said firmly. "As Christians and neighbors we need to help each other when trouble comes. If we can't lick a problem, we'll outlive it with God's help."

This time Mr. Trainer didn't turn away in anger. He listened with gratitude, then hesitantly began his story. When he finished, the two sat watching the autumn leaves cascade into colorful piles.

"I never thought I'd see any of them again," Ben told Papa. "I prayed every day and feel that God has forgiven me. Else I'd never have accepted Him publicly and attempted to help with His business in the church. You don't think I did wrong in that, Will?"

"Remember the Lord's companions and how human the disciples were," Papa reminded him. "Church members are only sinners saved by abundant mercy. No one is free of mistakes."

"But I should have used more judgment in choosing—companions."

"Keep praying. And I will, too. God will see you through this."

As much as he trusted God to solve the problem, though, Papa couldn't sit idly while his friend suffered. The next day he rode to town alone. He boldly entered the hotel looking for the pair who had visited Ben. The dark-eyed boy was alone in the room, looking out the window.

Papa walked toward him and placed a hand on his shoulder. "What's the matter, boy?" he asked.

The boy turned and looked at the floor a long moment. He slowly lifted his head.

"Uncle Alex has been at it again," he said in a low voice. He said his Uncle Alex had been arrested for making counterfeit money and would be returned to the penitentiary.

Papa knew there was only one thing left to do. He took the boy to Deep Valley and left him at Ben Trainer's where Ben and the boy could work out the remaining kinks in the problem.

Papa then lost no time hastening home to tell Mama everything. The way things were winding up he knew Ben wouldn't mind.

Mama was pleased over Papa's confiding in her. Then wide-eyed with wonder that something exciting had finally happened in our valley, she just had to have a hand in ending the story.

"I'm marching straight to Noreen to give her a piece of my mind," she declared. "To think that a sister of mine could be so devoid of compassion and feeling!"

On the way to her sister's house she met Ben Trainer and his newly adopted son heading in the same direction.

"I just had to try again with Noreen because of Will's encouragement," Ben told her. "She and I have a lot of other things to tackle."

His last sentence made Mama remember Papa's example. A "certain" feeling made her decide to let the main characters work out the end of the plot themselves. So she just turned around and headed back home where she belonged.

The next day Aunt Noreen couldn't wait to visit Mama. For the first time in months the sisters enjoyed a heart-to-heart talk.

After Uncle Ed's death when Ben came to see Aunt Noreen, the two had talked of their early days together when they were young. Ben told Noreen that he went West to forget her because he was heartbroken over her marriage. The pair shared other conversation, too, as he helped her with the store.

"Ben and I always had a lot in common and liked the same things," Aunt Noreen told Mama. "After Ed's death I was lonely and needed companionship and help. So Ben and I just picked up where we left off, I guess, until he said we couldn't marry until he confessed something. My heart turned over inside then, Betsey, because I sensed trouble edging around the bend."

"Um," Mama said, as she snapped the beans in her lap.

"When he told me how he'd met that cheap girl who lied about her folks, telling him she had no one in the world, I felt disgust rising in my throat. Ben then disclosed that he went through a fake marriage, not knowing until a week later that the girl was already married. He left her after he discovered this, of course, and she went back to her husband. Ben never knew she got pregnant and had his son. After hearing all this, I told him the whole business sounded like a cheap dime novel to me!"

Mama lifted her left eyebrow as she snapped the beans vigorously. "Um," she said again.

"He could count himself lucky, I told him, to get away from that low-down riffraff, losing nothing but the money the girl and her brother got from him and the desert space of Arizona land in which he'd invested. Yes, Betsey, I told him that in anger," Aunt Noreen confided in a low tone.

"That forsaken desert land isn't much like our green Kentucky hills, I've heard," Mama reflected, forgetting her work to revel in the wondrous autumn beauty of the mountains. "I would really miss our valley if I were stranded out there."

"Yes, Ben must have been very homesick," Aunt Noreen mused softly. "Yet he went on to Utah where the Mormons were kind to him and gave him a job. Thanks to them, he learned to be thrifty. So he saved to come back here, built up his farm, and started his own business."

"And to think he never knew he had a

son." Mama's hands remained idle as she
sifted her thoughts. "Anyone can see that
the boy is a carbon copy of Ben when
he was young."

"If only the girl and her brother hadn't
involved Ben in one of their counterfeit
deals," Aunt Noreen sighed. "When I heard
that sordid story of how he got raveled in
the deal even though he was innocent, I
told him I never wanted to be reminded
of such things again. I had no right to judge
him so, of course."

"You've always been too sensitive for
your own good," Mama chided her
youngest sister. "But here I go judging you.
Noreen. . . ." She smiled suddenly. "Isn't it
a blessing that God, instead of us, passes
the supreme, final sentence?"

Aunt Noreen returned to the story. "As
for the girl's real husband, his worst fault
was his drunkenness. He had no part in
the counterfeiting. Too bad he fell down
the canyon. And the mother of the boy
died three years ago, Ben said."

"The brother has spent these last five
years in the pen," Aunt Noreen said. "And
as soon as he is released, here he starts
counterfeiting again. He decided to get
revenge on Ben for testifying against him."

"It's just too bad that he'd try to use the

boy for blackmailing purposes to ruin Ben's
standing in the community." Mama put
away her pan of beans, now that she and
her sister had reviewed the story to their
satisfaction.

"He'll not ruin Ben. And he'll never have
a chance to lay hands on that boy again!"
Aunt Noreen affirmed. "He's mine and
Ben's along with my nine. Ben and I are
getting married next week, and as far as I'm
concerned, everyone is welcome to hear the
whole story. It's best to bring news out in
the wash and let the neighbors accept us
as we are."

Mama smiled at her sister. Then she
walked to her kitchen window to smile up
at God. "It must be a comfort to You, Lord,"
she said softly, "that we earthen vessels can
iron out a few wrinkles in our relationships
with each other. It will save You a mite of
work when we step into heaven."

At the wedding, Papa stood as best
man for the deacon who had dropped the
collection plate when he'd seen a counterfeit
bill and recognized it. The next Sunday,
Papa and Ben, his new brother-in-law and
lifetime friend except for two days, walked
side by side up the church aisle to take up
the collection.

# The Bad Girl in Our Valley

"Some folks make a hobby out of judging their neighbors!" Mama declared vehemently in a moment of exasperation. "More people are run down by gossip than by these new cars on the street."

Of course she herself could not refrain from gossiping a slice or two, the same as the other women around her. But when it came to lowering somebody's reputation down the well, she wouldn't stoop to such a thing.

"If everyone swept his own doorstep, then the whole wide world would be clean," Mama quoted an old proverb. "If we remembered that, we'd be so busy housecleaning our own souls that there would be no time to darken the character of others."

When Selda Simms went bad, many people took time from work to devote to their favorite hobby. It kept some busy for years. Their warmed-over repetitions were the reason for Mama's present exasperation.

Selda was sturdy and efficient. Her plain face, tanned by summer sun, resembled a broad, toast-colored sycamore leaf. When we used to play house at school, her huge arms reached out in an expansive manner as she played the mother to us younger girls.

"Guess I can take care of all ten of you," she assured us with warm maternal concern.

Selda's father had died when she was eight. After that her mother had shut herself up in her room away from society. Never one to share ideas and recipes like the other women, Minnie Simms grew more withdrawn than ever after her husband had been killed on the railroad.

"Lanse Simms was probably drunk at the time," more than one person surmised, using the only muscle that shows no fatigue.

Mama said nothing. She put on her second best apron and went down to help and comfort Minnie.

But Mrs. Simms didn't take to comforting, from either Mama or anyone else. And so she died comfortless after Selda had waited on her hand and foot for years. Selda was around seventeen when her mother ultimately gave up the effort to live.

For Selda, though, living, despite misfortune, couldn't be defined as an effort. She always appeared in love with life. As she fingered blue morning glories after a dew-drenched night, she seemed to have discovered the essence of beauty. When trailing snow fluttered down, she'd let the flakes nestle where they would, caressing the ones on her old black jacket. As she observed and appreciated all beauty, her happy eyes conveyed rays of wonder to others.

"The need to behold the loveliness about her is as necessary as food to Selda," Mama remarked once. "Happiness unrolls in unexpected moments for her. It isn't to be created once and for all and held in trust like money in the bank. Rather, happiness for Selda is to weave small rainbows daily for herself and others."

After her mother's death Selda stayed with Big Tim Henson, Elijah's brother, and his wife. As usual Big Tim's frail, little, ever-complaining wife was ailing again. He hadn't been able to find any hired girl to suit her or any medicine to help her.

"Something other than a physical ailment

is wrong with Jean," he had told Papa.

Papa said that when Big Tim had said that, he'd looked as if he might burst out crying. Jean sometimes reminded him of Minnie Simms, Big Tim said, except that when she withdrew from society, she talked all the time about things that didn't make sense.

Of course Selda didn't please Jean Henson long. Selda went to live with the Sands family awhile and then got a job at a store in town.

She worked around two years. When she stopped, naturally there was speculation about the reason. Eventually the neighbors discovered the answer to their curiosity— Selda was going to have a baby.

Our valley was horrified! Having a baby out of holy wedlock was the most dreadful sin one could commit, according to the belief of some. And for Selda Simms to stoop to this crime—someone whom we had held in high esteem—well, that was too much for most valley folk.

But not for Mama. When Selda was ostracized and hardly anyone would go near her in those last months, Mama went even more often just to help with the heavy work. The baby was born in October.

"A honey-colored mass of hair above two

tiny azure eyes. That's the baby for you,"
Mama disclosed, when she returned at five
in the morning after the delivery.

So the baby favored Selda, everyone
agreed, with that taffy hair and blue eyes.
Many were disappointed, because they
couldn't discern who the father was. Of
course in the long run it didn't actually
matter. Selda was the fallen woman and
deserved all the blame bestowed on her.

"I've often wondered," Mama said at that
time, "if people who whisper bad things
about others have sometimes entertained the
idea of doing the same thing themselves."

"Betsey!" Papa said.

For months before the baby's birth,
Selda had been despondent. Her happy,
contagious laugh had flown like milkweed
pods in a September wind. Her step was
no longer carefree and eager to make
discoveries. Her merry eyes seemed closed
to the beauty of nature around her. She
remained like that until her daughter,
Melita, was almost two years old.

Meanwhile, other events besides Selda's
sin provoked conversation. The earliest
spring on record tripped into Deep Valley; a
new family moved in; and Big Tim Henson
made his quarterly trip far beyond our hills
to the city where his wife had been in a

mental institution for four years. The day
he left, Mama, Papa, the boys, and I worked
on a new henhouse.

We were nailing boards on the west end
next to the honeysuckled rock cliff when
we saw Selda Simms enter our yard. She
led Melita by the hand and stopped beneath
an apple tree.

She knelt to pick up an apple blossom
and held it under Melita's tiny nose. In that
moment Selda started to mend the torn
garment of her life. Her face came alive with
remembered joy. Her eyes radiated delight
with the flowers as she surveyed their long-
forgotten loveliness. They had become
rainbows of hope and promise once more.

I looked at Mama as she held a nail
suspended in the air. A sudden
comprehending look dawned in her eyes.
Only much later did I learn that when
Melita's blue eyes had surveyed the beauty
of the flower, Mama had known instantly
who her father was. A certain look in the
child's eyes had betrayed the truth.

The look had held a particular blend of
joy and sorrow. Mama knew only one man
whose eyes contained a lonely look of
indefinable sadness intermingled with joy.
How that could have been transmitted to
a child, Mama didn't know, but she had
recognized the look.

From that day on, there was a change
in Selda Simms. More mature, she didn't
return to her youthful manner of expressing
delight. Now, if she beheld a butterfly, she
didn't run after it hastily like a child
touching its radiance. Instead she would
stop to point out its beauty to Melita.
Together the two would then enjoy it from
afar as if realizing that if the butterfly were
caught and held, the wondrous dust of its
tiny form would fade and its glory would
be diminished for others.

Gradually our valley began to accept
Selda once more. Still, there were some who
found it difficult to forgive; those continued
to condemn and greet Selda with a pasted-
on smile. Mama used to wonder if such
people ever stopped to consider little sins of
their own—like biting remarks or unforgiving
spirits. These sins were a hindrance
in walking the path to heaven, too.

"Jesus surely didn't uphold sins of the
flesh," Mama said. "He told the woman
taken in adultery to go and sin no more.
Selda has done as He admonished. She's
repented of her sin, most surely, and
accepted her child in all humility. I
somehow feel that Selda will come to the
church before long if we will let her in."

The year Melita was three, new mines
opened in our valley; we added a new

Sunday school room to the church; and
Jean Henson died in the mental institution.
Big Tim brought her home and buried
her beside her parents. Alone in his old
farmhouse, as he had been for years,
he sat on his porch day after day.

A month after his wife died, he suddenly
married Selda Simms and took her and
Melita to his big house. Again tongues
clacked about "the bad girl in our valley."

"Why would a respected fellow like
Timothy Henson want to hitch up with
Selda?" was the repeated query. No one
seemed to know.

The Sunday after the wedding, however,
everyone was enlightened. Big Tim stood
up in church after the sermon and publicly
acknowledged that Melita belonged to him.
He knelt on his knees, asking forgiveness.
He had accepted Christ as his Savior,
he said, and wanted to become a
church member.

Like thunder after a flash of lightning,
shared looks over the room immediately
met in mutual questioning. Mental
arithmetic was used rapidly to count back
to the time when Melita had been conceived.
No, it couldn't have been when Selda was
staying at the Henson farm. It wasn't until
after Mrs. Henson had long been sent away.

Big Tim rose from his knees and I looked
at his eyes. In that instant I knew what
Mama had discerned that afternoon beneath
the apple tree. She'd known, as I did now,
that little Melita's eyes were an exact replica
of Big Tim's.

All eyes turned as Selda slowly walked
down the aisle. She knelt at the altar, her
shoulders slumped, her head bowed.

The room became silent as a tomb. After
a few moments she rose slowly, gave her
hand to Pastor Horne, and spoke to him in
a low tone. When he asked if the church
would accept Selda Henson as a candidate
for baptism, the room remained deathly still.

Amid the silence Ben Trainer cleared his
throat twice. He reached for a songbook and
in a hearty voice started singing, "What can
wash away my sin? Nothing but the blood
of Jesus. . . ."

With that, the atmosphere started clearing
like fog rising above the hills after a storm
in July. Everyone joined Ben in the song
and then launched into "Amazing Grace."
Before the service ended, people right and
left were crying and shaking hands with
Selda and Big Tim. This was the most
moving meeting we'd had in years,
everybody agreed.

"Tim must have been very lonely after

Jean was sent away," Mama told Papa
outside near our buggy.

Papa smiled down at her.

"Betsey," he said, "you have a warm
heart that wants to think the best of others,
even when faced with the reality of human
weakness and sin."

Yes, Mama had always been kind to "the
bad girl in our valley." She'd been kind to
Big Tim in his sorrow and need. With a
heart like hers she couldn't be otherwise.

She returned Papa's smile and walked
over to Mr. and Mrs. Henson, inviting
them to supper the next week.

# ❧The Pastor Who Ran Away from Church

While Mama stayed busy ironing out relationships among the neighbors, Papa thought of a plan to benefit his sons and the other boys growing up in our community. After reading about the Boy Scouts of America and the Boys' Clubs, he decided to start a Boys' Club.

Within a week he'd rounded up eighteen boys. Soon they were busy cleaning Grandfather's old barn, which hadn't been used for years. They planned to use it as the headquarters for their activities.

"And just what will be those activities?" Mama asked. "A club's no benefit without some worthwhile goals. Come to think of it, Will, you've been rather vague about them all along."

"I'm thinking," Papa said, heading for the barn.

"He's always thinking," Mama remarked

to me a bit tartly after his departure. "Well,
Jenny, the house belongs to us these days."

Three days later Papa's meditation
brought results. While the boys played
horseshoes, he and Mama sat in the swing
by the garden path. He began reading his
blueprint for future club activities. Mama
was elated that he was once again confiding
his dreams to her.

"I might have known that horseshoe
playing would be on the program." She
turned to watch her sons. "It's a good clean
sport and calls for competitive action."

"The game will develop the boys
physically and help them make decisions in
aiming for a goal," Papa added. "We can set
up competitive matches in the county fair."

"And you're starting a class in leather
work, too?" Mama questioned. "Perhaps
you can teach the boys to make belts and
billfolds like those you and Grandfather
used to make."

"Milton Tanner promised to start them
on baskets and chairs. Betsey, there's
something about the ability to create,
the joy one senses. It's something inside
us that stems from the Lord."

"I know," Mama said softly. "I feel that
way about making a home for you and our
children." She looked up at the sky. "Will,

just think what a supreme glow God must have sensed when He created man and woman and gave them talents to use."

Papa's list contained schedules of ball games for the boys and checker games they would supervise for the older men. That would please the aged persons, since so many spent self-pity, rather than money, on themselves. The list also included a reading program and a schedule for a bookmobile.

"Why, Will," Mama exclaimed, "you mean you'll lend your books and those your parents left you!"

"I can't possibly remember or share all the ideas I meet in books," Papa admitted ruefully. "So the neighbors must start reading for themselves."

"Grandma and Grandfather would be pleased mightily to share their books," Mama decided.

"We'll consider other projects as the situations arise," Papa commented hurriedly as he saw Kate Rankin coming up the road.

Kate pattered through the yard, smoothing her dust cap as usual. Her inquisitive sparrow eyes wondered what had been going on at the old barn in recent days. "I couldn't wait a minute longer to find out!" she exclaimed.

"Will Jennings," she said upon learning

the plans, "I've heard the limit now! You mean the boys will bring books around for us grown-ups to read? When can we find the time, I'd like to know, with all the work awaiting us?"

Despite Kate's workload, she was never too busy to lend a helping hand. Two days later Mama reached to take that hand. Aunt Noreen was having another baby, and planned to have the delivery in the new hospital in town. That was really an event, since she would be the first woman in our valley to give birth to a child there. Our women were shy about doctors and the new hospital; they preferred the neighborhood midwives.

Aunt Noreen's labor pains started on Saturday morning after Papa, Uncle Ben, and the boys had taken our buggy to town. Since Kate was the only woman around who could guide horses as accurately as a man, Mama quickly enlisted her aid. The trio set out hastily for their destination.

It was necessary for Aunt Noreen to give birth in the hospital because the doctor had feared complications. She might have twins, he'd said, and he didn't like the idea at her age. Late that evening Aunt Noreen was delivered of three tiny baby boys. With our valley making the headlines, we really had something to talk about now—triplets and all of them boys!

"We'll enroll them immediately in the Boys' Club," Papa commented lightly.

The next week Mama and Kate again drove to the hospital. Mama spent most of the time with her sister, but Kate visited the other patients, enjoying herself greatly while listening to their life stories. She lived and suffered with the patients and found nourishment from their joys and sorrows.

When Mama and Kate prepared for their return trip home, Kate could hardly wait. She had a slice of news that surpassed even the advent of the triplets, she told Mama.

"Never would I have imagined seeing that person in the hospital!" she declared, as she held the reins with one hand while checking the angle of her dust cap.

Nor could my family have envisioned who the person was when Mama disclosed the news to us. "Will, Kate found someone else she knows in the hospital—Stanton Trelawney—who took my jelly," she said, looking up at Papa.

"Stanton Trelawney!"

"Yes. And not even his brother, Jacob, knows that he's there. Jacob hasn't heard from him since he left here."

"But why is he in the hospital?"

Mama turned to me and the boys. "All of you may as well know. Everyone will learn before morning since Kate had a few errands to dust from her schedule, she said. Stanton tried to kill himself. He tried to cut the veins in his wrist, then his throat. Failed even at that, he said. I wonder what failure he's had before."

A week later Stanton went to his brother's house. Somewhat against Papa's wishes, Mama visited the Trelawneys several times. To her surprise she learned that Stanton Trelawney had once been a pastor who had become disillusioned about his beliefs. He'd given up his church because he couldn't reason his beliefs to his satisfaction. He had turned to peddling, then to drink, hoping to drown his doubts and guilt.

Even worse, he had almost stooped to thievery. As we knew, he had taken Mama's jelly, the first such act he'd committed. He'd hidden it, meaning to sell it later. But passing the church door on his way from our valley, he had suddenly sensed the old longing for the peace inside the sacred walls. Could he dare to stop a mere moment to see how it felt to be inside a church once more?

"Mrs. Jennings, I couldn't forget the day when you read the Bible," Stanton told

Mama. "As I watched you accept faith in such a simple manner, I began to see that trust and belief don't require a reason. After a long while I saw that the God you trust so completely is too big to comprehend the whole of. He is too omniscient for us to understand Him fully with our human eyes. That was my trouble all along. I was trying to borrow God's eyes to understand Him, the universe—and people."

"If we could comprehend God fully, He wouldn't be God. We need only to understand what we can of Him and the corner we occupy," Mama explained simply, "and to remember that the one true picture of life flows in the channel of love between Him and us."

"Lying there in bed, I meditated deeply on religion," continued Stanton. "Still, I had taken the jelly and had planned to join an escaped convict. Then with all my guilt, unresolved questions, and suffering, I stopped by the church. At the altar I thought of the labor your family and others had contributed in building the church. Churches contain flaws, as do all institutions, I know. Yet despite everything, they hold a certain atmosphere that isn't present outside their doors because the majority of the members, I believe now, truly want to carry out Jesus' teachings."

Stanton paused a long moment.

"There in the church," he said slowly, "I began to realize this. I saw that doubt is too lonely to realize that faith lies near as a next-door neighbor. I discerned, too, that I had never been an agnostic after all, nor an atheist, not even in my most doubt-filled moments."

"Churches . . ." began Mama, wasting no time in standing up for her convictions on the worth and need of organized religion. Five minutes later she wound up her exhortation on what she thought of churches, agnostics, and atheists.

"Stanton Trelawney, I've never yet heard of an atheist starting a home for orphans or traveling the second mile for others!" she declared.

She looked him squarely in the eye. "Now if you think there is something wrong with churches, your first step should be to settle your private relationship with God and ask forgiveness. Next, get involved in the church where you live and help it climb to maturity despite those who would tear down its walls."

A few weeks later Stanton took her advice, knelt at the altar for forgiveness, and joined our church. Standing before the pulpit, he told the congregation he wished to tell the story of his failure as a pastor.

The story awakened us to appreciate the simple way of life in our small isolated valley in the hills away from the big cities. We weren't perfect, since we were human and prone to error and sometimes became involved in unpleasant incidents. But we shared our lives with each other and talked out our problems and differences sooner or later. We stood by each other and didn't carry jealousy or anger to the extreme.

"Jealousy and anger may start over little things and reach the limit. Such divided my church into two factions," Stanton disclosed that day. "The division made me doubt God's presence and the worth of men. I relinquished my pulpit because I could no longer preach with those doubts in my heart."

He had been preaching in a small town when the wives of two deacons had disagreed on the position of the piano. The disagreement had then spread to a slight coolness between their husbands. One man ran a store on the east side of town; the other ran a store on the west.

Next, the two deacons had disagreed on a

new roof for the church. They even carried
the collected grievances into their business
lives, dropping nasty remarks among their
customers. The church members began
taking sides in the dispute.

"And to think that the whole thing started
over such trifles!" Stanton exclaimed. "'Is
this religion?' I asked myself. What was
wrong with my sermons that I couldn't
influence the members toward walking the
Christian path to heaven?"

He stopped to meditate. "Finally then,"
he said hesitantly, "one of the two deacons
accused the other—the church treasurer—of
taking church money. No one believed the
sordid tale at first but it was true. Meanwhile,
the guilty deacon tried to place the blame
on me. It was then that I ran away."

He concluded the unbelievable story,
revealing the details he'd already told Mama.

A few days later Stanton visited us. "I just
lost hold of myself when I let loose of God's
hand," he confided.

"All people grow lost without the guiding
hand of God," Papa said. "And you're not
the first person to grow confused over
human nature."

"After losing my faith, I literally swam
in the mire. It was as if I myself had to

participate in evil so I could understand
why men stoop to wickedness. Can you
understand that? I experienced to the depth
that, as Isaiah recorded, there is no peace to
the wicked. Can you see, too, how I grew
discouraged, even after I started groping my
way back?"

"Spiritual growth is often a matter of
stepping forward, stumbling, and rising to
walk again," Mama reflected. "Even St. Paul
had two factions warring in him. I guess
almost everyone senses little civil wars
inside at times."

"Humanity couldn't survive if God didn't
deal patiently as we stumble and fail,"
Stanton decided. "Our Creator is so far
beyond human nature. That's what makes
Him God, of course, as you pointed out
to me, Mrs. Jennings. If only I could serve
Him again."

"You'll return to the pulpit then?" Papa
asked.

Stanton shook his head. "No, I'm not
worthy. I must serve Him some other way."

A few days later Stanton began helping
with the local Boys' Club. He started a Bible
study course for the shut-ins and others
who didn't attend church. He began a
visitation program in which he helped

many to unravel their complicated home
lives and led three couples to accept
the Lord.

On a winter afternoon Mama and Papa sat
talking of Stanton Trelawney's renewed zeal
and faith.

"Stanton is carrying the gospel into homes
that he might never have reached as a
pastor," Mama said. "Dedicated laymen can
sometimes dig to the root of problems."

"He's a natural leader for the Boys' Club,"
Papa replied. "Trelawney isn't one to
talk religion on Sunday and the be
embarrassed to mention it on Monday.
He possesses a rare talent for discussing
spiritual values in such a natural manner
with the boys that Christ's principles come
alive for them."

"Oh, Will," Mama said fondly.

When Papa became engrossed in the
study of his left shoe, Mama knew that he
didn't realize that he could well be speaking
of himself.

The next day Mama observed two people
evidently engrossed in something other than
spiritual topics. Upon entering Uncle Ben's
grocery, she noticed Stanton Trelawney
talking with Kate Rankin beside the cracker
barrel. That spring Pastor Horne united

Stanton Trelawney and Kate Rankin, the thirty-six-year-old spinster, in marriage. After the wedding they left for the West to assume charge of a boys' home.

"Stanton will love those boys and teach them the love of God," Papa said positively.

"We can never thank Kate enough for saving John's life. She will be good for the boys too," Mama replied with satisfaction. "She'll be interested in their welfare and enjoy the details of their lives."

The raindrops outside the window trickled together like crystal drops of sugar syrup. Mama watched them and then turned to Papa. "One thing about Kate, she does plenty of living herself by being concerned about the lives of others, even if her interest does turn into gossip now and then."

Papa smiled as if to himself. Mama didn't stop to consider that she could be summing up a portion of her own character.

"Kate really grew interested in the bookmobile once she started reading biography," Mama commented. "She'll educate herself now that she's started."

"Kate's a determined woman," Papa said.

"Yes, and with grit to spare."

Mama laughed suddenly. "Will, do you

suppose Kate will wear her dust cap out West? The only time I ever saw her without it was on her wedding day."

"Betsey . . ." Papa said reprovingly.

Then, in spite of himself little crinkles of laughter began spreading from the corners of his eyes.

## ❧ Mama's Witness in the Five-and-ten-cent Store

Papa clung to the old ways he'd known as a boy growing up in a one-room log cabin at the head of Deep Valley. He had never owned a car, but in their aging years after my brothers and I had left home, he and Mama enjoyed riding into town with Uncle Alson in his car. Papa loved to walk up and down the streets greeting friends and stopping to talk or to read poetry to them. Mama liked to visit the Hobbs' five-and-ten-cent store.

In previous years when we children had needed things, Mama had rarely bought anything for herself, especially any luxury or even some trifle she wanted for no special reason. Even though she and Papa now had a few more dollars than in earlier years, Mama still couldn't break the habit of thinking twice, or maybe three or four times, before making a purchase.

She still wouldn't buy many clothes for herself, but she did love beads and pearl necklaces and bought them. She liked to spend time in the five-and-ten searching for bargains on thread, cloth, batting for quilts, and brightly colored yarn for knitting. She spent money on pretty stationary and on photo albums. Most of all, she spent money on birthday, sympathy, and get-well cards to send to friends and relatives.

Buying these items was one reason Mama liked to visit the five-and-ten-cent store. The supreme reason she liked to go there, however, was to meet friends and strangers who soon became friends, or at least passing acquaintances.

"Sooner or later everyone comes to the five-and-ten," she said.

As a rule, three or four chairs sat near the entrance of the store. To rest her tired small feet after making her purchases, Mama would sit in a chair as she waited for Papa and my uncle to get ready to leave town. Never one to waste time, she would lay her bundles on the floor beside her and fish for her small New Testament amid the clutter in her pocketbook. Not ashamed to read her Bible in public, she would start reading a favorite psalm or memorize one while waiting—if Papa and Uncle tarried long enough!

"You'd be surprised how much Bible reading you can get in while waiting," she told us more than once.

What Mama enjoyed most, though, were the occasions when people sat down beside her and joined her in conversation. Almost always she would find out their name, the name of their spouse, the names of their children if they had any, who their parents were, and even where their grandparents had come from. She would learn their occupation, where they lived, the type of home they had, their hobbies, and their favorite food.

Establishing a mutual bond of friendship by showing interest in their lives, Mama would then hold up her little New Testament, read a verse or two, and testify what God meant in her life. Her blue eyes reflected a glad, happy spirit which caused more than one person to listen and perhaps think of spiritual matters, rather than of the merchandise on the store shelves.

Some people passing by would stare curiously at her, perhaps wondering if she were trying to start a prayer meeting in the five-and-ten. However, some would stop to catch a Bible verse read in her soft lilting voice and then hurry on. Those listening a moment or so may have had their loads lifted, if only temporarily. Mama's Bible

reading perhaps gave them a lift of
the spirit.

There is no way of knowing, of course, if
her witnessing about the love of Jesus really
helped a great many people. Looking back
now, I like to feel that her words may
have had far-reaching consequences. Her
becoming acquainted with people in the
dime store, displaying an interest in their
lives, and witnessing about the love of
Christ in her own life may have helped lead
many to the Lord—if not at that particular
time, then perhaps in future years.

I do know of some, however, who were
grateful for Mama's witnessing and Bible
reading, for her using her time well while
she rested her feet.

There was the old gentleman edging
toward his eighties, all alone and feeling no
one cared for him. Mama would take time
to talk to him.

"Nobody has talked to him in a long
time," she told us. "I had time; he had time.
And so we shared conversation. Naturally,
I got around to telling him how much the
Lord means to me. He couldn't read and
had never read the Bible."

Mama found out where he lived, and
Papa started visiting him and reading God's
Word to him. Both Mama and Papa were

with the old fellow when he died a month later. He had professed faith in Christ the week before.

Then there was the tired, discouraged twenty-six-year-old mother of two small children, who had slumped down in the chair beside Mama when Mama had smiled at her. The girl disclosed that she and her husband had just had a fight and she'd left him. She was staying with her parents and felt she was imposing on them.

"Life is just a mess, one mess after another!" exclaimed the young mother. "Oh, what's the use? What's life all about anyway?"

Mama reached for the two-year-old and held the child on her lap. She smoothed the little girl's tangled blonde curls. "It's about love, dear," she told the child's mother softly.

"Love!" The young mother's voice was harsh. Two women passing by stopped a brief second, then hurried on. "What's love got to do with life? I don't believe in love anymore."

"But you must believe in love, dear. Why, love is the very core of life. Life started with God's love long ago," Mama explained as she began telling about God's love in first creating the world.

The girl's replies were cynical and she kept interrupting Mama. She stood up suddenly, holding her two-year-old and reaching for the little five-year-old boy's hand. She hurried out the door, but five minutes later she returned. Her eyes were somewhat less hard and stony.

"Say, I bet you've never had a cross piece of luck in your life, have you?" demanded the girl. "Guess you've lived on easy street all these years."

Mama's eyes twinkled. "I wasn't exactly born with a silver spoon in my mouth and haven't dined on a gold platter since," she replied.

The girl looked at her for one long moment. "I don't know what it is, but you're different somehow," she said slowly. "I'd like to have what you have, whatever it is."

That was the beginning. Mama learned that the young woman and her husband lived in a poor section at the lower end of town. For three Saturdays straight she and Mama sat and talked in the five-and-ten. The girl went back to her husband and Mama visited them, taking the children some clothes she'd made. The young husband didn't quit his drinking all at once. It took him five years and in that time his wife left him several times. Three times she came to stay with Mama and Papa. The story had a happy ending, though. The husband finally was converted and gave up alcohol. He and his wife were baptized in the Free Will Baptist Church.

"It was your doing," the girl told Mama on the day of their baptism.

"No, dear, it was God's doing. He works through us," Mama said simply.

There were also others whose lives Mama influenced for the good. Among them were the blind lady whom Mama had helped when she'd dropped her purse and who thereafter came to the dime store on Saturdays to discuss the Bible with Mama, and the twenty-year-old girl who discovered she had diabetes and felt so discouraged. And there were still others who came and found a listening heart directing them to the Lord. The young man who had quarreled with his father. The boy who had quarreled with his sweetheart. The secretary who couldn't get along with her boss. The man whose wife wouldn't stay home with their children, and the teacher who simply couldn't stand the schoolroom a minute longer!

No matter what their age, they talked to Mama and with God's guidance she helped them. They all became her friends and kept up the friendship through the years. Eventually all but one became Christians and joined churches of various denominations.

As she'd sit in the dime store, Mama would sometimes watch the cars go by on the street. This fast way of traveling is different from the old horse and buggy days, she'd muse, recalling the steamboat whistles on the Big Sandy River when she was a little girl. She remembered seeing the first train come to Pikeville.

The town had grown with its many new stores, houses, and churches. In the old days the Primitive and the Old Regular Baptists had been about the only church groups in the hills. Mama still had a warm spot in her heart for them since she had grown up with their beliefs. They had kept spiritual values alive in the mountains until other groups rode in to establish new churches. Now the town and the little hollows and creeks could lay claim to many churches of varied denominations. When a stranger sat by Mama, she would tell him about the available churches and say that he would be welcome in all of them.

"I don't like to advise people on what church to attend. I tell them the churches are waiting for them," Mama said. "And I let people talk out their lives and problems to me. When they've spent their words, I then try to tell them what it takes to shoulder life—to repent of their sin, kneel with their load of care, and let God carry the burden."

Such was Mama's witness of God's love and the plan of salvation in the five-and-ten-cent store.

A friend once asked me why my mother spent so much time in the dime store. I thought a moment and then replied slowly, "She's listening to the burdens of others. She's giving them the right medicine to start them walking toward heaven's highway."

# 🌷 Mama
# Dreams of Heaven

By the time Papa died of a heart attack at sixty-one, Mama had seen many of her generation step from earthly life into eternity. Her two babies, Jettie-Elizabeth and little Willie, had been with God many years. Her parents were long since dead, and other relatives and friends were gone.

With death ringing the doorbell so often, Mama came to accept death as she did life. The two companions composed the universe, she said, since they walked side by side visiting everyone.

"Now that so many of my people and friends have stepped across the threshold," she declared more than once, "heaven seems almost next-door. God may call me next."

Yet the years reeled from the calendar and Mama remained with us. As she left her seventies and enrolled in the eighties'

class, she was still in fairly good health,
kept her own home, and visited the
neighbors whenever possible, helping them
by her little acts of Christian love and
encouragement.

She spoke frequently, as the aged do, of
the departed. "I've outlived them all!" she
declared once in a sprightly mood. "And
I was the least in the family," she mused,
as she listed the exact weight, height, and
years of the Greenleaf clan.

In these latter years Mama's memory
remained intact. She still loved life and
creativity, and was an avid reader. With
leisure time at last, she read widely in
biography, fiction, and spiritual books. At
night she read her Bible, and though alone
now, she still held the family devotional
that she and Papa had started at their
marriage altar.

Every few days she took a "ginning" day
from her regular schedule, as she always
had, to examine her soul and share
thoughts with God. She talked to Him more
than ever now. God and heaven seemed
closer each day, and the communication
line kept opening wider for conversation.

As in the past, Mama still experienced
"certain" feelings. At least twice a week
she'd have a special neighbor on her heart.

That would call for a visit, of course, or a
phone call to check on the neighbor's
welfare.

"I'll still trudge the second mile when I'm
able," she told my brother Clayton spiritedly
one day when he objected to her traveling
in the cold weather. "You see, I won't be
walking the path to heaven long now," she
added. "I'll soon step over the threshold. But
I can't let God down while I remain here."

She looked down the valley road with a
dreamy look in her blue eyes. "Will used
to walk the second mile with me," she
recalled. "In fact, he walked it more often
and with more faith than I. He's walking it
in heaven now, of course, for service surely
awaits us there."

She lifted her left eyebrow in thought and
remained silent for some time. My oldest
brother turned to smile at me, and I smiled
back as we shared our thoughts about this
little mannerism of Mama.

"I dreamed an unusually vivid dream last
night," she said at length.

Clayton chuckled in his teasing manner.
"Mama, you were never one to dream
much. Why are you starting at this late
date? Papa was the one who used to read
his dream book and attempt to unwind his
dreams."

Mama smiled in remembrance, then grew serious. "In the dream I saw a beautiful green valley far more beautiful than Deep Valley. It was more lovely also than the Cypress Gardens." She paused, thinking of a recent trip to Florida with my brother Jerry and his family.

Two days later Mama grew ill, and for the first time in her eighty-two years was taken to the hospital. The doctor we called was surprised that she had never previously been admitted. She had never had a family doctor and had never taken any medicine except antacid tablets from the drugstore. Although she had Parkinson's disease, she had never taken any treatment and it didn't trouble her greatly.

But now at last Mama was truly ill and required special care. She had diabetes, we learned, and had to be on insulin. She became tired inside, as the elderly so often do. She grew despondent—something unusual for her—and feared she would die.

"It was the dream," she told us and everyone who would listen. "The valley I dreamed about was heaven. I'll be traveling there any day now."

With heaven beckoning her, Mama was surprised that she didn't want to leave earth after all. "Sure, I want to see Will and the

others," she said. "But I'll miss you children
so. Besides, I want to read a few more
books, piece another Kentucky garden quilt,
and attend church again. And I'd like to
visit Jim and his wife."

By her bedside, my brother John sighed.
I walked to the window to hide my tears.
Mama would never see the new home of
Jim, my third brother, who lived in
Tennessee, I felt.

That night Mama suffered a stroke. When
she could talk again, she didn't realize what
she was saying. Even the doctor gave her
up.

Surprisingly though, she grew better and
went home. We took turns staying with her
and having her visit us. She even traveled
to Tennessee to visit Jim. After that, she
came to stay with me awhile.

"Jenny," she said in my home one day,
"my dream about heaven is still real in my
thoughts. It'll come true any day now for
me." She smiled a weary little smile.

I laughed and teasingly said, "Oh, Mama,
stop saying that! You've been going to
heaven ever so long. And you haven't gone
yet."

Her eyes twinkled in her old way. "Don't
give up on me," she spoke in her spicy tone
of earlier days. "God opens the door an inch

wider each day, throwing out another
braid from the welcome mat. Moreover,
Jenny . . ." her voice sank low, "I see your
father almost every day now. He has a
suitcase in his hand and stretches out his
hand to me. But I won't go with him."

"Mama, stop that right now!" I
commanded. "You give me an eerie feeling.
You're dreaming again."

"Yes, I dream about him all along. But I
see him, too, in daylight. Every time I come
here to your house, he follows me back
down the road when I go home."

"Mama, it's that diabetes, the insulin,
or the new medicine you're taking for the
Parkinson's disease. At any rate, stop
talking so."

"And I even saw Stanton Trelawney and
Kate one day." She laughed suddenly. "Kate
wore her dust cap, as usual."

With effort I restrained an answer. Kate
and Stanton Trelawney had been killed
three years before in an auto accident
out West.

Mama talked, too, of seeing her mother,
Aunt Careen, and her dead brothers. She
spoke often of my little brother and sister,
who had died before I was born.

"God always gives something for that
which is taken from us, though," she

affirmed. "When they died, He sent Jim, Jerry, and you."

One day while she was staying with me, I found her crying when she awoke from her nap. "I dreamed of that little boy," she said.

"What little boy?"

"My little boy," she replied impatiently, as if I should know.

Yes, she was talking of little Willie again. I looked at her, a frail old lady in her eighties, speaking of the baby she'd held in her arms as a beautiful young mother. **Personality and the person never die,** I thought. Nor do personal relationships. Linked with love in Christ, these are eternal.

"He was playing with other children. I called to him but he wouldn't come to me." Again tears rose in Mama's eyes.

That night I sat thinking a long time about her asserting so often that she saw her departed loved ones.

"No matter what anyone says about the effects of medicine, old age, or relived memories," I concluded, "I believe, after these experiences with Mama, that as one nears eternity, he is reaching to those in heaven and they may be beckoning to him."

The following spring Mama, Clayton, Jerry, and I were sitting in her parlor bedroom. Again she warned us of her entrance to heaven at any moment.

We spoke of Nathaniel Finklehoffe, the Jewish boy who'd tried to hang himself on our ancient clothes rack. Nathaniel, working for the Salvation Army, had since led many to Jesus Christ. "The bad girl in our valley," whom Mama had befriended, was now a devout Christian and leading in the church bus ministry. Jonah Malone, who found his wife's teapot to use as a tithing one, was the Sunday school director. Elijah and Melanie Henson headed the youth group in the church and taught a class in flower appreciation at our new recreation center.

"You helped all these, Mama," said Jerry. "That should be worth a few stars in your crown when you enter heaven."

Mama sighed. She seemed so tired. "I don't expect stars, son. I merely want to occupy a little corner of eternity beside Papa."

"And just look at us, Mama." Clayton's eyes twinkled as hers often did. "You had a hand in putting us where we are today."

The bright old twinkle suddenly leaped into Mama's eyes. "I'll say I did! I brought you into the world. I'm proud of you, Clayton, teaching religion in that big college. And, Jerry, you're the best young doctor in the town clinic, of course."

She turned suddenly to look out the window. Then folding her tiny, wrinkled hands on the windowsill, she smiled up at the sky and spoke softly as if to God alone.

"They've all done well, Lord, with Your help, mine, and Will's. Jim is a fine Methodist pastor in Tennessee. John is an effective preacher in our new Baptist church here on Pinnacle Mountain. And Jenny is spreading Your love through her writing, Lord."

She lifted her left eyebrow in thought and then sighed softly. "I've stumbled along on my feet of clay, but the children and others have been a credit, You know. What would life be without children, relatives, and the neighbors, Lord? Surely we'll have neighbors in heaven, won't we?"

My brothers and I slipped quietly from the room to let Mama continue her conversation with God.

The next morning we found her with a faint smile on her face, her left eyebrow lifted as if facing the ultimate in thought.

Mama had finally, as she'd predicted so often, taken the last step on her pathway to heaven.